The Encyclopedia of CARS

VOLUME THREE – Du Pont to Hudson

The Encyclopedia of
CARS

VOLUME THREE – Du Pont to Hudson

Chelsea House Publishers

Philadelphia

Edited by Chris Horton
Foreword by Karl Ludvigsen

Published in 1998 by
Chelsea House Publishers
1974 Sproul Road, Suite 400
P.O. Box 914
Broomall, PA 19008-0914

Printed in Italy

**Library of Congress Cataloging-in-Publication
Data**
Encyclopedia of Cars/edited by Chris Horton:
foreword by Karl Ludvigsen.
     p.   cm.
    Includes indexes.
    ISBN 0-7910-4865-9 (vol. 1)
    ISBN 0-7910-4866-7 (vol. 2)
    ISBN 0-7910-4867-5 (vol. 3)
    ISBN 0-7910-4868-3 (vol. 4)
    ISBN 0-7910-4869-1 (vol. 5)
    ISBN 0-7910-4870-5 (vol. 6)
    ISBN 0-7910-4871-3 (vol. 7)
    ISBN 0-7910-4864-0 (set)

1. Automobiles–Encyclopedias. I. Horton, Chris.
TL9. E5233 1997   97-17890
629.222 03–DC21   CIP

Page 2: Fiat Bravo 2.0 HGT
Page 3: Honda CRX
Right: Ford F-150 Lariat Supercab

Contents

Du Pont

U.S.A.
1920–1932

E. Paul du Pont's manufacturing philosophy was to build high-quality cars in limited numbers; in the event his company built no more than 537 vehicles of all types during its 12-year lifetime, based initially in Wilmington, Delaware, and from 1923 in Moore, Pennsylvania. The very last cars were assembled and the Indian motorcycle factory in Springfield, which du Pont had acquired.

The first Du Pont was powered by a 4.1-litre four-cylinder sidevalve engine of the company's own design and manufacture, but this soon gave way to proprietary six-cylinder engines, initially made by Herschel-Spillman. Several different body styles were always available, too, built mostly by Merrimac, Waterhouse and Derham, and in touring, saloon, speedster and cabriolet configurations.

For 1925 the Model D was fitted with a five-litre six-cylinder Wisconsin straight-six producing 75bhp, a four-speed constant-mesh transmission and Lockheed hydraulic brakes all round. Its successor the Model E, was available with a supercharger if required, then in July 1928 came the Model G, arguably the best Du Pont of all and, in its distictive Speedster bodywork, certainly the best-known.

The Speedster was not a particularly good-looking car, however. It had a long, smooth hood behind a grille that concealed the radiator (the latter a pioneering feature), narrow wings or cycle-type mudguards, and Woodlite headlamps which, even if they did relatively little to illuminate the road ahead, certainly set the car apart from its contemporaries. Two- and four-seat versions were available, as well as a more conventionally styled roadster on the same chassis.

In 1931 the Model G was succeeded, logically enough, by the Model H. Mechanically, this was virtually identical to the Model G, but had a slightly longer

wheelbase to accommodate the flamboyant touring body with which the only three cars to be assembled were fitted.

By the end of the year falling sales had brought the company to the brink of bankruptcy. Manufacturing high-quality cars at unashamedly high prices paid off during the 1920s but the Depression brought that to an end and Du Pont, with no cheaper models to fall back on and what it saw as a reputation to protect, closed its doors for good in January 1932.

Left: 1929 Du Pont Short Roadster
Below: 1929 Du Pont Touring
Bottom: 1930 Speedster with unique radiator

Above: 1930 Model G Royal town car

The Model G was the car which made the marque of Du Pont famous and its 5.2-litre straight-eight engine, which gave it a top speed of well over 177km/h (110mph), was just one of a series of sophisticated touches which ensured that the few able to afford one would appreciate this fine automobile.

Duryea

U.S.A.
1893–1916

One of the earliest car manufacturers in America, the company was started by two brothers, Charles E. and J. Frank Duryea. Charles began his first motorized horse-buggy in 1891, but utilized Frank's mechanical skills to complete it, returning to his bicycle sale and repair job in Peoria, Illinois. This led to a long-running argument over whose invention it was!

The second prototype (Frank's work) appeared in 1895, winning the 50-mile (80-kilometre) *Chicago Times Herald* race in nine hours, and two years later the Duryea Motor Wagon Co. was formed in Springfield, Massachusetts. The brothers controlled two-thirds of the shares between them, the remainder held by local investors. Cars were also built in Peoria, where Charles still worked, by the Duryea Manufacturing Co.

By 1898 the brothers had split, Frank

Above: One offshoot included Stevens-Duryea like this 1911 model

going to the Automobile Co. of America and then to Stevens Arms in 1901, which was to produce the Stevens-Duryea. In 1906 he designed a six-cylinder engine which was claimed to be the first of that type in America. Charles formed the Duryea Power Co. in Reading, Pennsylvania, continuing to manufacture the Duryea, which by this time were a variety of three- and four-wheeled vehicles with tiller controls.

The following year Henry Sturmey began building British Duryeas under licence in Coventry, which lasted until 1906. The marque was also made under licence at Waterloo in Iowa and Liège in Belgium during the period from 1899 to 1908.

In 1908 the company moved to Saginaw in Michigan, changing its name to the Duryea Motor Co. Charles, having built a three-cylinder rotary-valve model in 1907, then brought out a successful high-wheeled buggy which was listed for the next six years. He tried a Duryea cyclecar in 1914, which was actually manufactured by a Philadelphia company, Cresson-Morris. Also built in Philadelphia – by Duryea Motors Inc. – was the Duryea-Gem of 1916, which was to prove Charles Duryea's last car. He died in 1939.

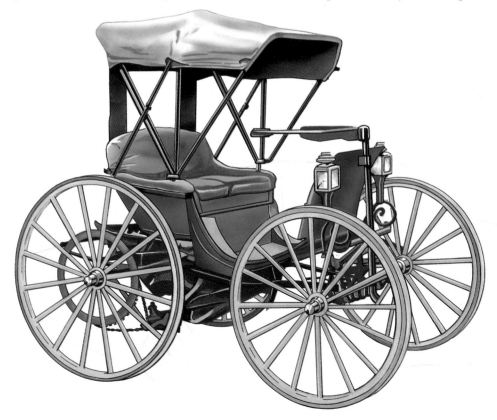

Though this high-wheeled buggy of 1893 looks primitive today, the Duryea company were actually remarkably successful for their time. This model boasted a 4hp two-stroke engine and friction-drive transmission.

Excelsior

Belgium
1903–1930

Engineer Arthur de Coninck set up a modest workshop in a Brussels garage towards the end of 1903. He gave the enterprise a grand name, the Compagnie Nationale Excelsior, which it would eventually live up to, becoming the premier Belgian make alongside Minerva.

To begin with, however, de Coninck produced a range of unremarkable vehicles using French engines designed by Aster, for whom de Coninck was also the Belgian agent. Within four years he was offering three vehicles of differing engine sizes, still using Aster units. In 1907 he acquired larger premises in Liège, forming La Société Arthur de Coninck et Compagnie. At this point de Coninck also began manufacturing his own power units and transmissions.

Two years later de Coninck expanded

Below: A 1928 Imperia Monte Carlo rally car

again, this time when he bought a factory at Saventhem previously owned by the Belgica company. The name was changed to Société des Automobiles Excelsior and the first six-cylinder model, the D6, was launched from there in 1910.

De Coninck's interest in competition saw an Excelsior team entered in the 1911 Coupe des Voitures Legères. Joseph Christaens drove six-cylinder cars in the 1912 French Grand Prix. After the war they had some notable successes in Belgian endurance races and also competed at Le Mans.

Excelsior began exporting to Britain and

Above: A cabriolet on an Excelsior chassis

France where the marque was popular up to the beginning of World War I. During German occupation de Coninck was deprived of his plant machinery, starting completely from scratch in 1919, although using modified D6 engines.

This was followed by the successful and prestigious Adex C, which became Excelsior's sole model. By 1927, however, the company's fortunes were failing, and it was taken over by Impéria. The marque's last public appearance was at the Brussels Salon of 1930.

Facel Vega

France
1954–1964

The name Facel was derived from Forges et Ateliers de Construction d'Eure et Loire S.A., set up in Paris in 1938 by Jean Daninos.

The company made machine-tools for the aircraft industry and under German occupation during World War II turned to manufacturing gas generators for cars.

After the war, production of aircraft-related equipment resumed and Facel made de Havilland gas-turbine components.

The company branched out and also manufactured kitchen furniture, office equipment and car bodies, mainly for Simca and Panhard.

Production of car bodies peaked in 1952 at more than 100 a day. The following year Panhard stopped using Facel but Simca bodies were made until 1961.

Daninos' own car was launched at the Paris Salon in July 1954. He called it the Vega and it was based on a prototype resembling the Ford Vendôme.

It used a 180bhp 4.5-litre De Soto Firedome V8, derived from the Chrysler Hemi, had drum brakes and tubular chassis.

The car was expensive for its day and most models were exported. A total of 46 were sold in 1954 and 1955.

The car was redesignated the Facel Vega in 1956 with a 5.4-litre engine. Later, the HK500 offered 350bhp from its 6.4 litres.

Production of a convertible in 1955 did not even reach double figures because of rigidity problems and the 1957 pillarless Excellence had similar problems – although more than 150 were made.

The compact Facellia of 1960 was a disaster, mainly because of its unreliable and noisy 1.6-litre engine designed by former Talbot man Carlo Machetti.

Daninos' last Facel was the Facel II, based on the HK500. It was a potent car but came at a time of serious financial problems.

A receiver was appointed in 1962 despite support from Mobil, Pont-à-Mousson and Hispano-Suiza.

The Volvo-engined Facel III was launched in the spring of 1963 but proved a vain attempt at a revival.

Later that year, S.F.E.R.M.A., a subsidiary of Sud-Aviation, was given a one-year management contract to rescue Facel.

The FV6 was launched with the six-cylinder Healey 3000 engine, reduced in capacity to fall within the French domestic 15hp tax cut-off. But after producing fewer than 30 cars, S.F.E.R.M.A. declined to renew its option.

The original company was declared bankrupt in 1965.

Top: The HK500, a 1958 model
Centre: The Facel II boasted even more power
Bottom: 1960's Facellia was an unsuccessful small car attempt

The Facellia was Facel Vega's attempt to go downmarket and build a smaller-engined car. Though pretty in the firm's distinctive way, production problems and reliability queries over its four-cylinder 1.6-litre engine prevented its success, and less than 500 made it to the customers.

Ferrari

Italy
1940 to date

Enzo Ferrari – the man behind one of the world's most famous names in exotic sports cars – was born in Modena, northern Italy in February 1898.

He became interested in motor racing after seeing his first event at the age of 10 and was driving the family car by 1911.

His father's railway-equipment manufacturing business was extended to motor repairs but tragedy struck in 1916 when his brother Alfredo was killed and their father died. The following year, Ferrari joined the artillery, initially as a farrier and then working on aero-engines.

He was invalided out in 1918 and made a vain attempt to get a job with Fiat. However, Ferrari found work with a Bolognese engineer called Giovanni who was converting small trucks to saloons and sports cars.

Ferrari was friendly with racing driver Ugo Sivocci and he got Ferrari a job test-driving for Construzions Meccaniche Nazionali in Milan. And this led to his first race, competing for CMN at the Parma Poggio di Berceto hillclimb in 1919.

Ferrari's enthusiasm for racing was fired and a year later he joined Alfa Romeo as a test-driver, finishing second for Alfa in the Targa Florio.

Above: 1948 Ferrari Type 166 Corsa Spider – priceless

Below: The 250GTO, the last of the Ferrari front-engined competition cars, was developed to overcome problems with the GT models, better stability at high speeds being one. During its 1962 season the GTO came second and third at Le Mans.

Ferrari enjoyed several wins, albeit minor, at the Circuit of Savio and earned the congratulations of Count Enrico Baracca, father of flying ace Francesco Baracca.

The famous pilot had been killed in 1918 and his mother, the Countess Paolina, dedicated her son's prancing-horse emblem to Ferrari. He adopted it as his badge.

Ferrari's racing career ended abruptly when his son Dino was born in January 1932. He decided to retire after being plagued by illness including a nervous breakdown in 1924.

During his racing days, he moved closer and closer to building his own cars. He left Alfa in 1929 and formed Societa Anonima Scuderia Ferrari as a limited company with partners Mario Tadini and the Caniato brothers, in Modena.

The company was mainly involved with racing Alfas. Alfa went into state ownership in 1932 but Ferrari carried on independently and was also involved in motorcycle racing.

Alfa formed Alfa Corse in 1938 with Ferrari as manager but the latter left a year later after a dispute with Spanish engineer Wilfredo Ricart. He used his golden handshake and the residual assets of Scuderia Ferrari and formed Societa Anonima Auto Avio Construzioni Ferrari. At first, the company concentrated on tool manufacture but soon began making racing cars.

The first car was called the 815 but the four-year Alfa severance conditions prevented him using the name Ferrari. It was designed by Alberto Massimino and built between December 1939 and April 1940. It featured a straight-eight engine, using some Fiat parts, with a Touring of Milan body.

Top: Sports car perfection – a 1950 166MM Barchetta
Above: 1951 Vignale Berlinetta, a more sophisticated 212 Export

The Daytona, styled by Pininfarina, was the last of the front-engined V12 Ferraris and when it was introduced in 1968 it was one of the fastest road cars ever with a top speed of 282km/h (175mph). Few have beaten that claim to this day.

Two of the cars showed promise in the Brescia Grand Prix but both retired before completing the course.

World War II halted production and Ferrari turned to making aircraft parts and machine tools. In 1943 he moved to nearby Maranello and, despite two bombing raids on the factory, it was rebuilt in 1946 with Ferrari announcing that he would build cars for both the road and track. By now, he was allowed to call them Ferraris.

The new breed was launched with a 1½-litre V12 racing sports car, designed by Gioacchino Colombo and announced in November 1946. It made its debut at a race in Piacenza in May 1947.

Three 125s were built and then came the larger-engined 159 and 166. It was the 166 which was to form the basis of the first road-going car – the 1947 166 Inter.

Ferrari's first customer took delivery in January 1948 and then Ferrari offered the 1951 195 Inter and the later 212 model.

Although road cars were still something of a sideline, Ferrari sold over 250 Inters plus the bigger-engined 342s and 375s for the American market.

Ferrari's enterprise and flair caught the imagination of Milanese businessman Franco Cornacchia and Luigi Chinetti, both of whom injected cash into the company and helped set up America's long-standing Ferrari connection which saw Briggs Cunningham import the first of the marque, a 1949 Spider.

The Americans demanded the biggest engines and fastest cars and, with few exceptions, opted for the 400 and 410 Superamerica models of the mid-1950s, the lightweight 410 Superfast and, eventually, the 4.9-litre 500 Superfast with a 400bhp engine.

In fact, the 500 was the last of the large but comparatively crude cars made specifically for the American market from 1964 to 1966. Thereafter, export cars to America were ostensibly European models doctored to comply with local legislation and sales requirements.

Ferrari owed much of his success to racing and the marque made its Formula One debut in September 1948 in the Italian Grand Prix at Valentino Park, Turin. Raymond Sommer – part of a three-car team – finished third.

The first Formula One win came the same year at Lake Garda, with Froilan

Above: The 250MM of 1953, another sleek coupé
Below: A 1965 Ferrari 500 Superfast

Below: 1969's 365GT 2+2
Bottom: The 206GT Dino of 1968
Overleaf: 1960 Ferrari 250 SWB

Above: A luxurious 2+2 coupé, the 250GT

Left: The 1965 275GTB 'shortnose' Ferrari

Below: The BB series – named Berlinetta Boxer, the body style and the engine layout – kept the company's name on the lips of cognoscenti during the early 1970s, and kept the firm's reputation firmly intact through a number of changes in engine size and upratings of performance.

Gonzalez taking a Ferrari to its first Grand Prix win in Britain in 1951. The car was designed by Aurelio Lampredi who had rejoined Ferrari two years earlier. A Ferrari also won the Mille Miglia in 1951 and the cars went from strength to strength, so far taking world championships nine times, nine Le Mans wins and close to 100 individual wins in Formula One.

Ferrari's son Dino was a talented engineer and played a prominent role in developing the V6 racing engine which bore his name. Tragically, he died in 1956 at the age of 24.

Ford of America had long since been keen to win Le Mans to boost its sporting image and tried to buy out Ferrari in the early 1960s. Ferrari backed out when he realized that he would lose control of his racing operations – the one part of his company which had always been near to his heart.

Instead, he preferred to stick with a deal clinched in 1955 when he agreed to take over the struggling Lancia Grand Prix team with Fiat financially supporting his own team.

Ferrari had already established a fine reputation with the 250 Europa of 1954, a true GT which committed his company to road car manufacture. Production really got underway with the three-litre 250GT in 1956. And the 1961 250 range included the Lusso (which means luxury) and the 250GT 2+2, the first Ferrari with more than two seats.

Lightweight versions were made available, called Berlinetta (little saloon). And in 1962, Ferrari introduced the short-chassis 250GTO – for Gran Turismo Omologato – and only 39 were built until 1964.

In the mid-1960s, production had increased significantly and Ferrari used the Fiat connection to the full. But one project was less than successful. Ferrari developed a four-cylinder engine intended for a small touring car. It was tried in a Fiat 1100 chassis but the project was dropped because Ferrari did not have the production capacity. The engine design was sold to the De Nora family who used it to build the ASA Mille in 1964. But the car never found popularity and production ended in 1967.

The phenomenal Pininfarina-styled

Top: 1967's 275 GTB/4
Centre: Competition cars were Ferrari's forte, like this 250 GTO Berlinetta

Above: The 250GTO of 1962, very much a road racer

front-engined V12 365GTB4 Daytona was introduced in 1968. With a top speed of 281km/h (175mph) it is still one of the world's fastest production cars.

The same year saw the launch of the Dino 206GT, developed from the 1965 206GTS racing sports car. It was a direct competitor to the Porsche 911 and used a Ferrari-designed engine built by Fiat. The familiar prancing-horse emblem was missing. Instead, the car bore a Dino badge, in memory of Enzo Ferrari's late son. The Dino later came with a larger engine in the 246GT and 246GTS Spider.

Ferrari introduced his first road-going V8 engine in the Bertone-styled 308GT4 in 1973 but reverted to Pininfarina for the 1975 308GTB.

Above: 1971's 365GTS4 Daytona Spider
Below:The 208 Turbo was one of the firm's first applications of turbocharging to their familiar Berlinetta body style. It gave the already awesome power of the beautifully engineered Ferrari engine a further boost.

Top: The 1975 Dino 308GT/4 2+2   *Above: The 308GTB of 1976*

Left: 1973 Dino 246GT Spider
Above: 1973 365GT4 2+2

Below: 1972 Daytona 365GTB4

Grand Prix racing had a major influence on the 365GT4BB Berlinetta Boxer. The flat-twelve engine was mounted amidships, first as a 4.4-litre unit and then in five-litre form. The latter was known as the 512BB, signifying cubic capacity and the number of cylinders.

The 1984 GTO was a homologation special, developed from the 308 series and built as a road car, but only in sufficient numbers to satisfy the requirements of racing regulations. The Boxer was replaced by the Testarossa, a road car capable of 290km/h (180mph).

Ferrari was never complacent about his cars and he continually uprated them with larger engines for the 308 and Mondial and

The Testarossa – the name means 'red head', a reference to the colour of the cam covers, and was used in the 1950s too – has become a byword for all that is desirable in the world of high-performance motoring. Few have had the opportunity to drive one, however, and' even fewer have tried its fabulous 290 km/h (180mph) top speed.

Top: 1979 400i Auto   *Above: The BB 512 of 1979*

Above: The formula did not arrive until after 1975's 365BB
Left: More racing technology in a 1982 quattrovalvole (four-valve) Mondial
Below: 1984's Testarossa

more power for the luxurious 400i. The 308 spawned the 3.2-litre 328 in 1985, which was superseded by the new 3.4-litre 348 GTB in 1989; the 400 evolved into the 412 in early 1985.

In 1987, he announced what many enthusiasts regard as the finest Ferrari ever – the F40. It was to be his last contribution to the world of exotic cars. Enzo Ferrari died in 1988 at the age of 90, but his memory – and his cars – live on.

Right: The Mondial 8, introduced in 1981
Below: A 1988 Mondial 3.2 2+2
Below right: The civilized 412 Auto

The Ferrari F40, launched in 1988 to celebrate the firm's fortieth year of car production, is capable of 322km/h (200mph) and in the hands of an expert driver can do awesome things. Formula One ace Nigel Mansell has a party trick of spinning one in its own length using power alone. Zero to 97km/h (0-60mph) takes four seconds, but the waiting list even at astronomical prices is rather longer.

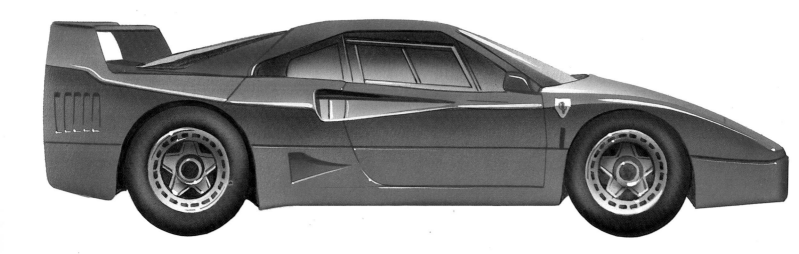

Top: 1984 Mondial Cabriolet Q/V   *Above: A 1988 F40 prototype*   *Below: 1989 Ferrari 348 ts*

Above: 1996 F355 Spider

Below: 1997 Ferrari 550 Maranello

Ferrari did not replace the 412 until 1992 when it launched the far more beautiful 456GT. Its smoother, well-balanced lines showed more than a hint of the classic 365GTB Daytona, but, with a 442bhp V12 under the hood, it could show a clean pair of heels to that seventies supercar as well as seat four in reasonable comfort.

The 348 was replaced in 1994 by the 355. Its new version of the classic Ferrari V8 engine had five valves per cylinder and produced a very healthy 380bhp. Its handling and ride was also improved over its predecessor, thanks to the use of high-tech, computer-controlled adaptive damping. Like the 348 it was available in hardtop GTB form and targa top GTS form but in 1995 a new bodystyle was introduced – the fully convertible Spider.

To celebrate 50 years of the famous marque, and as a follow-up to the great F40, Ferrari built the the F50. This Pininfarina-styled stripped-out road racer was as near as one could get to driving a Grand Prix car on the road. A 60-valve, 4.7-litre, naturally

aspirated V12 gave earth-shattering acceleration and a top speed of over 200mph.

By 1996 the old Testarossa, or 512, was getting distinctly long in the tooth. Ferrari replaced it with a front-engined two-seater coupé called the 550 Maranello. A rear transaxle was used to get even weight distribution. Its performance was not far short of that of the F50.

Below: 1996 Ferrari F355 Berlinetta

Above: 1996 Ferrari 456GT   *Below: Ferrari F40*

Fiat

Italy
1899 to date

The F.I.A.T. company was founded in July 1899 by Giovanni Agnelli, di Bricherasio and Count Carlo Biscaretti Di Ruffia. Of the three, the entrepreneur Agnelli was the leading light behind the early commercial success of the new firm.

Left: 1902 F.I.A.T. 8hp

Above: The first F.I.A.T. – 1899-1900

The first F.I.A.T. (*Fabbrica Italiana Automobili Torino*) was a rear-engined 3½hp flat-twin machine of 700cc capacity, based on a car produced by the Ceirano brothers. In 1900/1901 a similarly designed 6/8hp version was built. However, in 1901, a vertical-twin model was introduced, with the engine mounted at the front. In 1902 the capacity was increased from 1082cc to 1884cc, the new 8hp engine being cooled by a honeycomb radiator.

Larger engines soon appeared – a 3768cc four-cylinder unit was introduced

in 1902, followed by Mercedes-like units with the cylinders cast in pairs. Twin-cylinder engines were discontinued from 1903.

In 1904, in which year the company began to make pressed-steel chassis frames, notable new models included the 16/20hp, intended for town use, and the more sporting 24/32hp.

By 1905, the huge 60hp F.I.A.T. with a 10.2-litre four-cylinder engine was available.

Fiat (the full stops were abandoned in

Above: The huge 60hp F.I.A.T. of 1905   *Below: 1911 28.3-litre Fiat S.76*

1906) employed shaft-drive for the first time in 1907 on its 14/16hp, and in the same year an 11-litre six-cylinder model was introduced.

The company's advanced thinking in engine design helped it to success in motor sport and notable victories were achieved by Fiat driver Nazarro in the Targa Florio, Kaiserpreis and French Grand Prix of 1907.

Fiat survived the European economic crisis of 1907, and its technical innovation continued, combined with a general reduction in the sizes of the company's power units. A monobloc four-cylinder two-litre 10/14hp L-head engine was introduced in 1908, with four-speed gearboxes available from 1909. The six-

cylinder Type 5 models of 1908 gave way to four-cylinder versions from 1909.

Fiat was an early exponent of the use of overhead valves and overhead camshafts. The 10.9-litre racers of 1905 had engines of overhead-valve design, while the 10.1-litre 75/90hp sports car of 1911 had an overhead-cam unit, as did the 10½-litre S.61 and the chain-driven, 14½-litre Grand Prix car of 1912.

Fiat produced a number of cars with very large engines for use in competition – the 18.2-litre Mephistopheles ran at Brooklands in 1908, while the S.76 of 1910 featured a 26.3-litre four-cylinder monobloc engine, and was capable of over 212 km/h (132mph). By 1914, though, Fiat

Left: The 3½hp F.I.A.T. of 1899 was the company's first model. Based on a design of the Ceirano brothers, the twin cylinder, rear-engined car has vis-à-vis bodywork. The letters of the firm's name stood for 'Fabbrica Italiana Automobili Torino'.

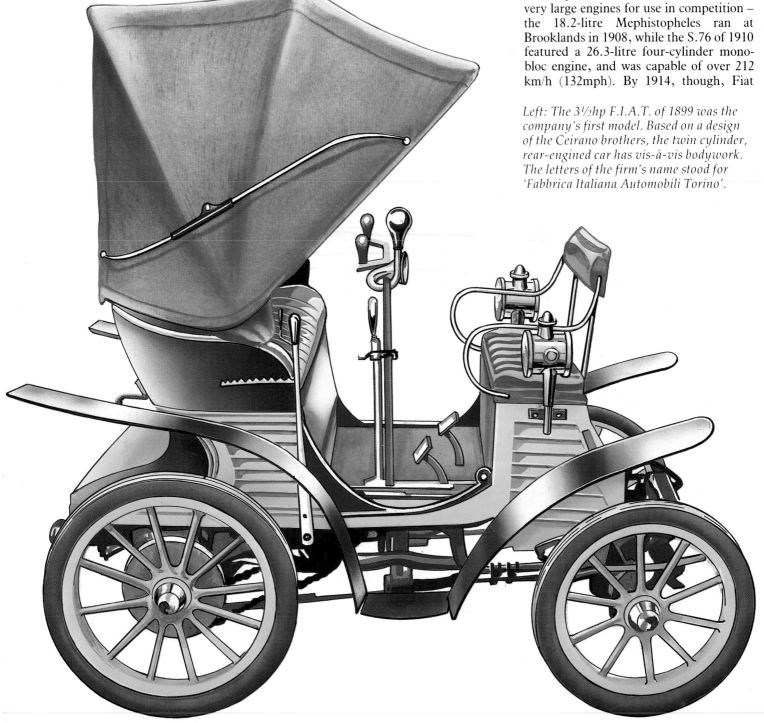

was extracting 135bhp from engines as comparatively small as 4½ litres.

A wide variety of Fiats were produced before World War I intervened. From 1910, the smallest Fiat was the 1844cc Type 1B, the intermediate range was known as the Type 2, and the largest, the 3964cc Type 3. Developments of the Type 3 included, in 1912, the models 3A and 3C, and the 4, with a 5.7-litre engine. In the same year the Type 5 (Tipo 55) again became part of the range, with a 60hp nine-litre engine.

A 3.9-litre six-cylinder Tipo 57 was also produced in 1911 and 1912 (only), while the 12/15hp model – a sports version of the Type 1B – was available from 1912.

The famous Fiat Zero, built between 1912 and 1915, was a solid 15hp four-seater, with a single-block engine, and although only 2,000 were built, it was an important model for the company.

By 1914, Fiat had streamlined bodywork designs, which now incorporated oval radiators. The larger cars had electric lighting and starting, and wire wheels – all advanced features for the time.

During the war, 35,000 vehicles were produced, including the 15/20hp Type 2B, and some Type 4s, for army staff use.

Fiat's mass-produced Tipo 501 was the first post-war model to emerge, in 1919. The car, with a detachable cylinder head and 1½-litre sidevalve engine, earned a reputation for reliability. Front-wheel brakes became optional on the 501 in 1925. The 501 was built until 1926, by which time some 45,000 had been produced. Larger models along the same lines as the 501 were introduced, with 2.3-litre four-cylinder and 3.4-litre six-cylinder engines.

Between 1921 and 1923, Fiat produced a very few Superfiats, which featured an overhead-valve 6.8-litre V12 engine, and

Above: A 6.8-litre V12 'Superfiat', 1921-22
Below: The 4.8-litre Fiat 519, 1922 on

brakes on all wheels. However, the model was dropped in favour of the 4764cc six-cylinder Tipo 519. This car, built until 1929, had a power output of 77bhp, and was equipped with hydro-mechanical servo brakes.

More angular styling and flat radiators were introduced with the Superfiat and the 519, the new bodywork being cheaper to produce.

In 1925 the 990cc overhead-camshaft-engined 509 was introduced. This proved to be a popular model, with some 90,000 produced in just four years.

Two new long-stroke six-cylinder sidevalve engines were introduced with the Tipo 520 and 525 models of 1927. The 520

Above: A 1913 example of the larger Fiats
Below: The 1.8-litre Fiat 1A, 1912-1915

Above: 1922 Fiat 501; body by Bean Cars
Below right: 1927 ohc Fiat 509

had large, American-style bodywork. The 525 was fitted with hydraulic brakes from 1930.

In 1932 another important small car was introduced by Fiat – the 508 Balilla. The little car had a short-stroke 995cc engine which gave lively performance, and the model featured hydraulic brakes. By 1934

Above: 508S Balilla Sport Spider 1933-37
Right: 1932 prototype Fiat 508 Balilla

the Balilla had a four-speed synchromesh gearbox and four-door pillarless saloon bodywork. An overhead-valve sports version produced 36bhp, and made the car very competitive in motor sport.

Fiat's Tipo 508S of the mid-1930s was an attractive machine which also performed well. Sleek bodywork with a long, louvred bonnet and slanted grille, plus cut-away doors, wire wheels and a 'finned' tail, gave the car a sporting air.

The larger 518 Ardita, produced with 1750cc and 2000cc four-cylinder engines, was introduced in 1933. The following year, the long-stroke six-cylinder 527 became available, and was produced for two years in a wide range of body styles.

From 1935, the Balilla was produced under licence by Simca in France, and by Polski-Fiat in Poland until the outbreak of World War II.

In 1936 Fiat introduced the 1500, a family car with a short-stroke six-cylinder engine, to the same bore/stroke ratio as the 508 Balilla. The 1500 featured Dubonnet ('knee action') independent front suspension and aerodynamic styling.

Fiat updated the Balilla in 1937, when the independent front-suspension 508C Millecento appeared. The 508C had a 1089cc overhead-valve engine developing 32bhp and giving the car a top speed of 112km/h (70mph). A coupé capable of 145km/h (90mph) and a long-wheelbase taxi version were also produced.

Of even more significance to the company was the 570cc Tipo 500A – the famous Topolino – which was introduced in late 1936. The tiny car had two-seater cabriolet bodywork and was powered by a four-cylinder 570cc sidevalve engine which was mounted in front of the radiator. The car also had independent front suspension, hydraulic brakes and a synchromesh gearbox.

The last large Fiat to appear before the outbreak of World War II was the six-cylinder, seven-seater 2800, of which only a few examples were built. After the war,

Above: Fiat's six-cylinder 1500, 1935-38
Below: The 500 Topolino appeared in 1936

Above: The 508C, sold from 1937
Bottom: 1951 Fiat 2800 Ghia

the sidevalve Topolino continued in production until 1948, when an overhead-valve version was introduced.

Updated 1100cc and 1500cc models, with steering-column gearchange, appeared in 1949, while in 1950 an overhead-valve four-cylinder 1400cc model was introduced. This advanced car featured unitary bodywork construction and 150,000 examples were built during its nine-year production run. Many variants were available during that time, including a diesel model, the cross-country Campagnola, and a 1.9-litre luxury version.

Fiat sports models of the early 1950s included the 193km/h (120mph) two-litre V8, and a 48bhp version of the 1100.

Above: The 500C Belvedere estate, 1951-55
Right: The Fiat Multipla of the 1960s

Below: Fiat's two-litre V8, 1952-54

The much-loved Fiat 500 gave way, in 1955, to another baby car, the rear-engined 600. The new model featured unitary construction and a four-cylinder 633cc engine developing 24bhp. The car sold in large numbers (a million had been built by 1950), and continued in production into the 1970s. An interesting variant was the Multiple, a large-bodied taxi/estate.

From late 1960 the 600 was fitted with a 767cc engine, developing 29bhp, and was designated 600D.

A new (Nuova) 500 was introduced in 1957, this time with a rear-mounted, air-cooled twin-cylinder 500cc engine, developing 16½bhp, later 22bhp. Giardiniera estate-car versions, built from 1960, had the engine fitted below the rear floor. Italy's favourite car, the 500, continued in production until March 1973.

Fiat's family 1100 continued in production throughout the 1950s and 1960s, in saloon and estate-car form, and was joined in 1958 by a 1200 Full-light saloon, and by 1300 and 1500 models in 1961. The saloon bodywork changed progressively from rounded styling to more boxy designs, while the roadster versions were particularly attractive.

From 1959, Fiat built six-cylinder saloons in 1800 (75bhp) and 2100 (82bhp) form, both versions having torsion-bar suspension at the front.

Attractive sports models of the same era included the Osca-engined twin-cam 1500 Cabriolet – this produced 90bhp and was capable of well over 160km/h (100mph). It was developed into the 100bhp 1600S model, capable of 173km/h (108mph).

A particularly fast Fiat, from 1963, was the 2300. Available in saloon, coupé and estate versions, the six-cylinder car produced 117bhp in standard form, and 150bhp in 2300S Coupé guise. Maximum speeds were 175km/h (109mph) and 190km/h (118mph) respectively.

A new rear-engined Fiat was to appear in 1964 – the 850, with a lively overhead-valve 850cc power unit developing 40bhp. The car was built in two-door saloon and (later) coupé form. Semi-automatic 'Idroconvert' transmission was available on the saloons. A Sport Coupé was introduced in 1965 and from 1968 it featured a 903cc engine developing 52bhp.

Two significant family models were

Top: Fiat's 1300 saloon of the 1960s
Above: 1963 150bhp 2300S two-door coupé

Above: Fiat 2300 Lusso four-door saloon
Below: The cute 500 was built until 1973

introduced in the mid-1960s – the 1197cc overhead-valve 124 of 1966, and the 1608cc double-overhead-camshaft 125, available from late 1967. The Sport Coupé version of the 124 had a five-speed gearbox and was powered by a 1438cc twin-overhead-camshaft engine, giving 96bhp and 179km/h (106mph). The 125 featured a 90bhp engine which endowed the car with brisk performance and a top speed of 160km/h (100mph) – excellent for a family car of the time.

The Fiat Dino Coupé, also introduced in October 1967, was powered by a Ferrari-designed, twin-overhead-camshaft, triple-Weber-carburettor V6 engine of 1987cc, developing 160bhp and giving the car a top speed of some 200km/h (125mph). The rear wheels were driven via a five-speed gearbox.

Fiat introduced two significant models in 1969. These were the front-wheel-drive

Above left: The 124 Berline, 1966 on
Above: Ferrari-engined Fiat Dino Coupé

128, in 1116cc and 1290cc versions (both overhead-camshaft engines) and the three-litre V6-powered 130 luxury saloon.

Fiat replaced the 850 with the front-wheel-drive 127 from 1971, the car being available in saloon and hatchback form, and with a 903cc overhead-valve engine and, later, a 1050cc overhead-camshaft unit. The lively four-seater 127 won the European Car of the Year Award in 1972, as had the 128 in 1970 and the 124 in 1967.

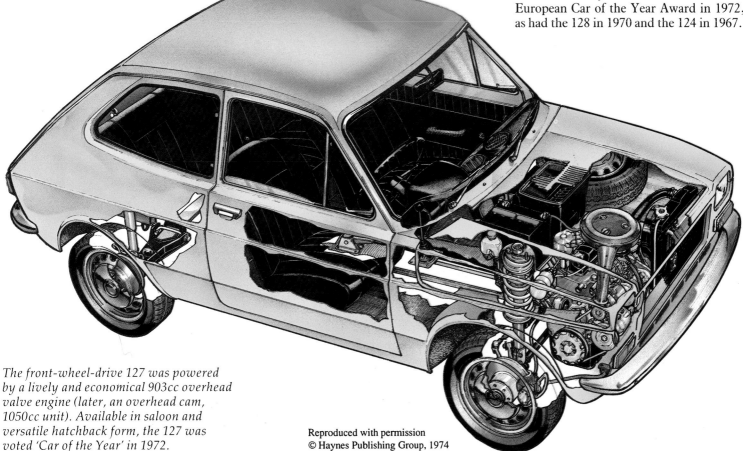

The front-wheel-drive 127 was powered by a lively and economical 903cc overhead valve engine (later, an overhead cam, 1050cc unit). Available in saloon and versatile hatchback form, the 127 was voted 'Car of the Year' in 1972.

Reproduced with permission
© Haynes Publishing Group, 1974

Above: Fiat's 767cc 600D of the 1960s
Above right: Fiat 128 estate/Sport coupé

The Fiat 126 was introduced as a replacement for the 500 from 1973. It had a 23bhp twin-cylinder engine of 594cc, and in early 1989 was still, in 126 BIS guise, the cheapest new car available in Britain.

Further Fiats to be introduced in the 1970s included the 132 in 1973 (the replacement for the 125) available in 1600 and 1800cc overhead-camshaft versions; the 131 Mirafiori, in 1297cc overhead-valve and 1585cc overhead-valve overhead-cam variants; from 1975 the 850-based 133; and the two-seater sports X1/9, introduced in 1977 and produced until 1989. The up-to-the-minute Strada

Right: 1976 111bhp Fiat 132 1800ES
Below: A powerful Strada 105TC of 1982

(Ritmo) family saloon was available from 1979, in 1100, 1300, 1500, 1600 (105TC) and 2000cc (Abarth 130TC) forms. The two-litre 132 saloon was sold from 1979.

The 1980s saw the introduction of the Panda, from 1981, initially in 903cc overhead-valve form, and later (from 1986) with 769cc or 999cc overhead-cam (F.I.R.E.) engines. The short-lived two-litre Argenta was available from 1982 to 1984.

One of Fiat's most successful models ever, the Uno (Car of the Year 1984) was introduced in 1983. Petrol engines ranged from 903cc overhead-valve types to 999cc, 1116cc, 1299cc, and 1301cc overhead-camshaft units. A 1697cc diesel was also

Above: The Croma hatchback, 1986 on

available. The Uno set standards for space
and fuel economy in small family cars of
the early 1980s.

*The Uno achieved the Car of the Year
Award in 1984. The three- or five-door
hatchback was available with petrol
engines from 900cc to 1.3-litres capacity,
or a 1.7-litre diesel. The tall bodywork
provided spacious accommodation.*

The Regata (saloon) and Weekend (estate) models were introduced in 1984, with a choice of 1.3-, 1.5- or 1.6-litre power, while the five-door two-litre Croma hatchback range was introduced in 1986.

The Fiat Tipo was introduced in 1988. Like the Uno, it was an innovative design in terms of space and overall design, and won the 1989 Car of the Year Award by a wide margin. The Tipo was powered by engines ranging from 1.4- and 1.6-litre petrol units to 1.7-litre and 1.9-litre (turbocharged) diesels. The Tipo's bodywork featured galvanized panels and a plastic tailgate to combat corrosion.

Above: A late 1980s Fiat Panda 4×4
Top right: A five-door Fiat Uno 70SL
Right: The Tipo – Car of the Year 1989
Below: The last X1/9 'Finale' model, 1989

Below: The Fiat X1/9 was a delightful mid-engined, two-seater sports car. Power was from a 1300cc or 1500cc overhead camshaft engine, mounted behind the cockpit. The cabin was comfortable, and the car featured two luggage compartments.

Above: 1990 Tempra SX

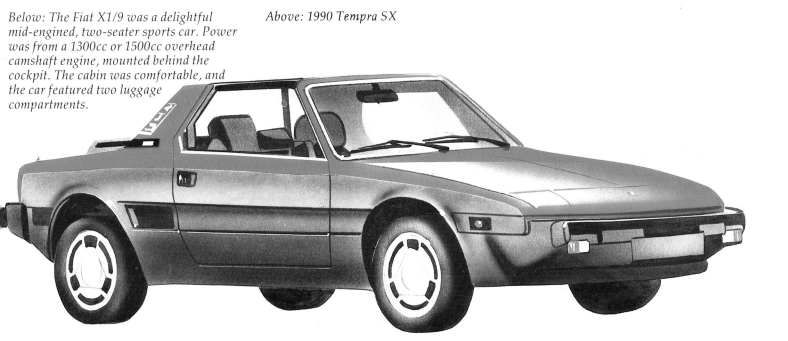

The new Tipo and Tempra helped Fiat enter the 1990s on a good note, and better was to follow. The improved build quality and design of these cars had changed the public's perception of the marque. Although some of the 1980s models remained in production, the Fiat range was almost unrecognizable by 1997.

The first new model of the 1990s was the Cinquecento. The name evoked memories of the famous Topolino and Nuova 500, and so did its diminutive size. It was built in Fiat's Polish factory and was launched at the end of 1991. An ideal town car, the Cinquecento boasted a four-seater, three-door hatchback body, extremely low fuel consumption and it cruised comfortably at 70mph. It was launched with a choice of two engines – the 899cc unit from the Uno and Panda and the two-cylinder 704cc water-cooled unit from the 126 BIS, although the smaller unit was not available in most markets. Its low price and minimal running costs made it a good seller, and the range remained unchanged until 1994 when the new Sporting model was launched. Using the 54bhp 1.1-litre engine from the Uno, the new model could reach 90mph (145km/h) and was great fun to drive. Alloy wheels, a sporty interior, spoilers and and bright colours made it the most desirable Cinquecento, with dealers unable to keep up with demand.

Fiat replaced the long-running Uno (although it was still made for the Polish market) with the stunning new Punto. This quirkily-styled hatchback was unlike anything else on the road and was even available with a six-speed gearbox on some models. As part of a new scheme by Fiat, the Punto was available in a multitude of different colours. Engines ranged from 54bhp 1.1-litre units, to a fire-breathing turbocharged 1.6-litre. As

Above: 1997 Fiat Marea Saloon

well as three- and five-door hatchbacks, there was also a cabriolet model.

Fiat's most stunning model for years also arrived in the 1990s. The new Coupé was styled in conjunction with Pininfarina and was almost more of a design statement than a mode of transport. To back up those stunning looks, the Coupé had more than adequate performance. Early four-cylinder 16-valve models were quick, but the later five-cylinder models, in particular the turbocharged version, could frighten Ferraris. The new five-cylinder engine produced 220bhp in turbocharged form and made the

Right: 1996 FiatBarchetta

Coupé the fastest car in its class with a 0-60mph (0-100km/h) time of 6.5 seconds and a top speed of over 150mph (240km/h).

The Coupé wasn't Fiat's only sports car though. The open-top Barchetta had less performance, but every bit as much style. Fiat's design centre created a well-proportioned retro-styled sports car which owed more to the original Alfa Romeo Spider, than Alfa's new Spider did.

Having done its job admirably, the competent, but ultimately bland Tipo was dropped in 1995. It was replaced by not one, but two cars, the Bravo and Brava. Identical under

Right: 1997 Fiat Coupé 20v Turbo
Below: 1996 Fiat Punto

The Marea, which used the new five-cylinder, was launched at around the same time and shared many styling features but was a bigger car to replace the Tempra.

Fiat also collaborated with Peugeot and Citroën to add a MPV to its range. Engines and a few minor styling tweaks set the Ulysse apart from the other companies' products.

Above: 1997 Fiat Marea Weekend
Below: Fiat Cinquecento Sporting

the skin, the Bravo was a 3-door hatchback, the Brava, a five-door notchback. Both benefited from Fiat's new-found innovative styling and some new engines, including the fine five-cylinder unit.

Left: 1997 Fiat Brava
Below left: 1997 Fiat Bravo
Below: FiatUlysse

Ford

U.S.A.
1901 to date

Henry Ford, who was destined to become one of the greatest industrialists of the twentieth century, completed his first car, or 'quadricycle', during 1896. A second was running by the summer of 1899 which sufficiently impressed his financiers to form the Detroit Automobile Company. Unfortunately, the cars failed to sell and Henry's ideas differed from those of the stockholders, so he left and turned to racing.

In October 1901 his newly completed 20hp racer won a 10-mile (16km) sweepstakes race at Grosse Point race track, Detroit, averaging 43.5mph (70 km/h). Ford gained favourable publicity from the event and secured further backing which led to the formation of the Henry Ford Company in November 1901. However, Ford's interests remained with racing and this led to friction. So after just three months he left with a U.S. $900 settlement, and an agreement that the company would change its name. This it ultimately did, to Cadillac.

During 1902 Ford teamed up with Tom Cooper and built two huge 80hp racers named 'Arrow' and '999' respectively, and enlisted Barney Oldfield as a competition driver. By all accounts the cars were brutes to handle, but Oldfield drove '999' to victory in the 1902 Manufacturers' Challenge Cup, completing the five-mile (eight-kilometre) race in 5 minutes 28 seconds.

Left: Henry Ford and his 1896 'Quadricycle'
Above: The first and the 10 millionth, a 1924 Model T
Below: A very early (1902) Ford

Henry Ford was, by now, well known and in a much better position to form a company that favoured his ideas, so, in June 1903 the Ford Motor Company was incorporated, and Henry could begin concentrating on producing an affordable car for the people. His mission to motorize the world had began.

The first car, the 1903 Model A, was a lightweight 8hp vehicle that could reach 30mph (48km/h). From the outset the company made a profit, U.S. $36,957 during its first 3½ months, and sales for 1903 totalled a respectable 1,708 cars.

Below: The 30mph Ford Model A of 1903

In 1904 the company offered the B, C and F models, and sales soared to 8,729 units. The Model N appeared in 1906 and proved a very good low-price car. More models followed: the R and S, essentially costlier versions of the N, and the six-cylinder K which replaced the B. The big K, advocated by Ford's partner, Alexander Malcolmson, just did not sell and was discontinued. Ford would not offer another six-cylinder car until 1941. Nevertheless, sales for 1906 reached an impressive 14,887 cars. Ford, having bought out other shareholders, now owned 58.5 per cent of the company.

Above: The Ford N (1906) preceded the 'T'
Below: The Model N sold for U.S. $600

One of the most significant landmarks in motoring history occurred on 1st October 1908, the day Ford launched the Model T. Henry Ford's (and the Model T's) success lay with his implementation of mass-production methods beginning in 1914, and the use of interchangeable precision parts, in an era when many other cars were still virtually hand-built. Ford's Highland Park, Detroit, factory was at the time the largest and most modern in the world. The company soon reaped the rewards for its efficiency and low unit costs, and Ford began cutting the price of his cars. In 1911 a Touring model cost U.S. $950, but by 1925 it was down to just U.S. $290, yet

Above: 1909 Model T Roadster
Right: 1911 'Australian' Model T Ford
Below: Cranking a 1910 Model T into life

Right: 1914 Model T

Top: Ford's six-cylinder Model K of 1906
Centre: 1909 Ford Model T Touring
Above: 1910 Model T on tour in 1967

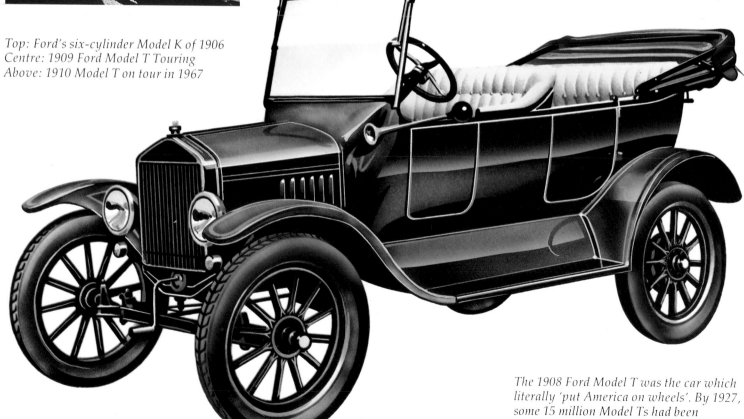

The 1908 Ford Model T was the car which literally 'put America on wheels'. By 1927, some 15 million Model Ts had been produced, all essentially similar. During 1923 alone, some 1.8 million were sold!

Ford was still averaging a U.S. $50 profit per car. Profits for 1923–24 stood at U.S. $100 million.

Apart from his customers, Henry Ford also shrewdly managed his workforce and, in 1914, introduced the celebrated U.S. $5, eight-hour working day. During this period Henry Ford became the most well-known and admired car manufacturer in the world.

Above: A distinctive 1912 Model T
Below: Timeless elegance – 1912 Model T

Top: Ford's first moving assembly line at Highland Park, Michigan in 1913
Above: 1915 Model T with twin spare tyres
Below: 1915 Ford Roadster on the 1964 Glidden Tour

Above: 1914 Ford Touring, filmed in 1964
Below: 1914 Model T wood bed pick-up

By 1926, however, Model T sales were flagging, in spite of subtle improvements and the availability of colours other than black for the first time in ten years. An increasingly unpopular aspect of the Model T was its outdated planetary transmission, which required a pedal to be held down to engage the low-speed gear or reverse. Also, as road conditions in the U.S.A. improved, customers began favouring refinement and comfort above unsophisticated raggedness. At first, Henry Ford, once so in tune with

motorists' requirements, would not accept that times were changing. However, even he could not ignore falling sales, and Model T production finally ended in May 1927.

The task of retooling for a new car was an enormous one, which took several months amidst much public speculation about the Model T's successor. It was not until December 1927 that the all-new Model A, a four-cylinder car, was finally

Above: 1915 Model T Touring – on tour!
Right: 1916 Model T Touring
Below: 1916 Model T Roadster

The Ford 18 V-8 of 1932 was developed from the Model A. The 3.6-litre V8 engine produced 70bhp and gave lively performance.

revealed to an eager public. The chassis, similar to the T, now featured a conventional three-speed transmission and four-wheel brakes. The styling, under the direction of Henry's son and company president, Edsel Ford, resembled the contemporary Lincoln (Ford having bought Lincoln in 1922). The Model A was immensely popular, and in January 1929 production worldwide totalled 159,786 units for the month. Ford was back on course.

Top: The popular Model A of 1928
Above: Model A Station Wagon

Above: 1928 Model A Tourer
Below: 1929 Model A Roadster with dickey

Above: 1926 Model T Tourer ('Swedish')
Below: 1926 Ford Roadster climbing hard
Bottom: 1928 Model A Sport Coupé

Below: 1930 Model A Roadster, hood up

Below: 1930 Model A Roadster, hood down!

March 1932 was another Ford landmark, when Henry Ford took a gamble in the midst of the Depression, and launched the first low-priced V8-powered car. Luckily, the gamble ultimately paid off, and the sidevalve flathead V8 remained Ford's primary power plant until 1953. Initially for 1932–33, the four-cylinder engine remained available. In 1937 a small-capacity V8 became optional which was subsequently replaced by a new sidevalve six in 1941.

Left: 1931 Ford Model A Convertible Sedan

Above: Stylish 1932 V-8 Roadster

Below: A De Luxe Phaeton Model A, 1930

During the 1930s Ford lost the number one sales spot to Chevrolet. This was partly because of Henry's adherence to transverse springing and outdated mechanical brakes; and partly because he alienated potential customers by his admiration for Hitler, and refused, sometimes by violent means, the unionization of his workforce.

An event that marked the end of an era for the company was the untimely death of Edsel Ford on 26 May 1943, aged 50. Edsel was very well liked and respected, and brought much to the Ford Motor Company. He made his greatest impact in the Lincoln division, and on the body styling of the Model A and V8 lines, all areas where his father showed little personal interest. Though always in his shadow, he had qualities that his father lacked, primarily fine taste and foresight.

Henry Ford, now nearly 80, and becoming increasingly eccentric, was re-elected as president while a power struggle between two key men – Charles Sorensen and Harry Bennett – went on beneath him. Bennett persuaded Ford that Sorensen, wanting to succeed Ford as president, had to go. Sorensen subsequently left to become president of Willys-Overland.

The instability at the top at Ford worried the U.S. government as Ford was a major contributor to the war effort. So, in August 1943 and aged just 26, Henry Ford II (the oldest of Edsel's three sons) was discharged from the U.S. Navy and named executive vice-president shortly after. Henry Ford was eventually persuaded by his family to resign as president in favour of Henry II in September 1945. With Henry gone the infamous Harry Bennett was on his own, and was edged out of the company the same month. Henry Ford died on 7th April 1947.

Right: 1957 Fairlane 500 Skyliner
Below: 1949 Custom Coupé

Immediately after the war the company was in turmoil, and losses ran as high as U.S. $10 million per month. Henry II was acutely aware of the situation and quickly brought in young blood and new ideas. He also knew that the first all-new post-war car had to succeed if the company was to survive. Fortunately, the 1949 Ford, the Custom Deluxe Tudor, announced in June 1948, did sell well, and the company finances rapidly returned to the black.

From 1952 Henry II set out to put Ford back in front, ahead of Chevrolet, by instigating a price-cutting war. By the mid-1950s Ford had managed to match Chevrolet model for model, but could not win the sales battle. The real losers were the small independent manufacturers: Hudson, Nash, Packard and Studebaker. They could not afford price cuts, consequently bankruptcies and mergers followed.

Above: 1955 Thunderbird

Above: 1953 Victoria Tudor HT
Below: Country Squire of 1954

Above: The 1957 Edsel Corsair

Above: The Mustang of the 1960s was a (relatively) small car, with sporting appeal, and was available in Hardtop, Fastback Coupé and Convertible versions.

Above: 1958 Edsel Pacer
Below: Fairlane 500 of 1958

Above: 1958 two-door Ford

Below: 1962 Falcon Station Wagon

Below: 1964 Galaxie 500 XL

In 1960 Henry II launched the compact Falcon range, and appointed Lee Iacocca as division general manager. Iacocca became the inspiration behind the Mustang and Ford's 'Total Performance' projects during the 1960s (before 'performance' became a dirty word in the industry), culminating with the legendary Shelby-Mustang GT 350/500 and Boss 302/429 series.

Above: Thunderbird, 1966   *Below: 1966 Ranchero Squire*

Below: 1974 LTD Brougham Hardtop   *Bottom: 1977 Pinto*

In the early 1970s the oil crisis left U.S. car manufacturers with whole ranges of largely obsolete cars, as the market swung towards economical Japanese and European cars. By 1980 the world was in an economic recession and Ford began losing vast sums of money, nearly U.S. $3.3 billion by 1982.

Fortunately for Ford, as the 1980s progressed and the company's rationalization and modernization plans took effect, things began to improve. The swing back into profit was well and truly made with the launch of the popular mid-sized Taurus range of cars in late 1985 and the aerodynamically-styled Thunderbird two years later. General Motors, on the other hand, was still struggling, and in 1986, for the first time since 1924, made less money than Ford.

Ford made a U.S. $3.7 billion profit in the first nine months of 1987, and looks well set as the company heads towards its centenary in 2003.

Above: 1972 Mustang two-door Hardtop
Below: Thunderbird, 1974; 460 c.i.d.
Bottom: 1977 Mercury Monarch Ghia

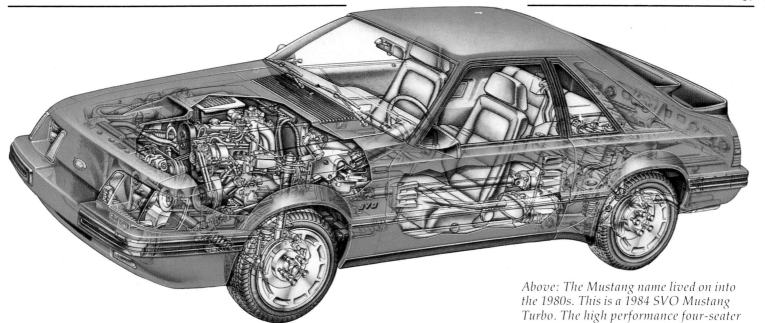

Above: The Mustang name lived on into the 1980s. This is a 1984 SVO Mustang Turbo. The high performance four-seater Mustangs of the mid-1980s offered a choice of power units

Above: Mustang II Ghia, October 1977

Above: 1980 two-door Fairmont

Above: 1980 Granada Ghia four-door sedan

Below: The 1989 Mustang was an unsophisticated but fast performer. It retained the classic front-engine rear-drive layout employed in Mustangs dating back to 1964.

Top: 1988 all-wheel-drive Tempo
Above: 1988 LTD Country Squire Wagon

Above: 1988 Thunderbird Coupé
Below: 1988 Mustang Convertible

Top: 1988 Aerostar; Eddie Bauer model
Below: The 1.3-litre Festiva, 1988
Bottom: 1989 Mustang Convertible

Ford was the only member of America's Big Three car manufacturers to get through the recession of the late-1980s without serious losses. The top-selling Taurus was a lesson to rivals and Ford's efficient manufacturing methods helped keep costs down. The company's Atlanta plant was the most efficient in the U.S., besting even the newest Japanese factories, with each Taurus taking under a minute to build. This efficiency helped Ford compete with the low-cost Japanese imports and kept the company afloat during the hard times.

Further increase in efficiency, and future stability, was gained by the company's 'Ford 2000' plan. This global reorganization of the company was intended to consolidate all its worldwide automotive units into the global Ford Automotive operation. By doing this, Ford could develop a new generation of world cars, vehicles it could sell all over the world with a minimum of modifications. These world cars could slash development costs, although there was some doubt as to how successful the plan would be. Would a car designed for German autobahns work as well driven within America's restrictive speed limits? The first true Ford world car was not expected to arrive until 1999.

Ford's small cars of the 1990s, the Aspire (Mazda 121) and Escort (Mazda 323) were developed in conjunction with Mazda (Ford owns a 25 per cent share in the Japanese company), as was the Ford Probe, which was

Top: The 1996 Ford Taurus SHO was the high-performance variant

Above: 1997 Ford Contour, was a Ford Europe Mondeo

Left: The Ford Aspire was based on the Mazda 121 or Kia Pride

Below: The U.S. -market Ford Escort was based on the Mazda 323 from 1990

more or less identical to the Mazda MX6 under the skin. Other cars were Ford through and through, with the medium-size Taurus an American sales chart success.

The mighty Mustang was replaced in 1993. Despite its modern and aerodynamic lines it still had the necessary horsepower under the bonnet and a very muscular stance. The GT model certainly had the muscle to match the looks. Its 4.6-litre V8 engine produced over 300bhp and could propel the hot Mustang to 60mph (100km/h) in under 6 seconds. The 3.8-litre V6 version was rather slower. It was also available in cabriolet form.

The Thunderbird name was kept alive in a new luxury sports grand tourer launched in 1988. The new smooth coupé styling had drag coefficient of only 0.31. With the 208bhp V8 engine it could top 130mph (210km/h).

Above: 1997 Ford Thunderbird

Left: Ford Probe

Far left: Ford F150 Lariat Supercab

Below left: 1997 Mustang GT

Below: Ford Explorer

Bottom: 1997 Ford Crown Victoria

Ford Europe

France
1947–1954

French Fords built before World War II were known as Matfords, following an agreement with the Mathis company, drawn up in 1934, under which the latter company was to produce only Ford vehicles. However, a few Fords were built in France prior to that – the Tracfords, which were essentially front-wheel-drive versions of the 8hp Model Y.

The Matfords were American in styling and origin, and featured V8 engines. The smallest engine was a 2.2-litre unit developing 63bhp. The models achieved some success in motor sport, notably in the Monte Carlo Rallies of 1936 and 1938.

The V8s continued to be built until 1939, the cars featuring vee-shaped windscreens from 1938. Their appearance was similar to that of the 22hp V8 British Ford.

In 1947 the company became known as Ford S.A.F. and the first Ford Vedette was introduced. It was fitted with the pre-war 2.2-litre V8 engine, and had an independent front suspension and hydraulic brakes. It remained in production until 1954.

In 1952 the V8-powered Comète coupé became available, with neat bodywork by Facel. A larger, 3.9-litre sidevalve engine was available from 1954. From 1955 the model was built on unitary-construction principles, and had an uprated (80bhp) engine.

Simca took over the company from Ford in late 1954 and continued building the Comète under the Simca Vedette name.

Right: The Taunus models of the mid-1970s were generally similar to the equivalent British-built Cortinas. With roomy bodywork and a range of engine sizes, they gave a wide choice to buyers. This is a 1976 example.

Germany
1931 to date

The first Fords to be assembled in Germany were Model Ts in 1925, followed by Model As from 1927. After the building of a new factory in Cologne, the German company built Model Bs under the name Rheinland, and the Model Y 8hp, known in Germany as the Köln.

The V8 engine was also built in Cologne, as were the 1157cc Eifel and the 1172cc Taunus from 1939. This car, with a sidevalve power unit similar to that used in the British Ford 10, was also built after World War II.

During the 1950s all the German Fords were known as Taunus models, and four-cylinder cars under 12M, 15M and 17M designations (denoting engine capacities; 12M indicated 1200cc) were produced.

The would-be Cortina competitor, the front-wheel-drive 12M of 1962, had a V4 engine, as did the larger-capacity 15M version. In 1964 the rear-wheel-drive 17M also used a V4 engine, of either 1.5 or 1.7 litres capacity. The 20M of the same year was powered by a two-litre V6 engine. By 1968 a 108bhp 2.3-litre V6 engine had been developed, for installation in the 20M RS.

From the late 1960s Ford of Cologne built its own versions of Fords also built in Britain and elsewhere, for example Escorts, Cortinas, Capris, Granadas and Sierras, often with minor variations in body styling and sometimes using its own V4 and V6 engines (notably in the Capris).

Right: 1975 (German) Granada Ghia Coupé

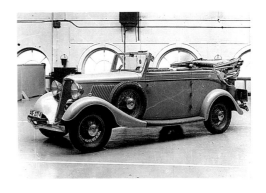

Above: 1933/4 Rheinland
Below: 1936/7 V-8 Type 48 Standard

Great Britain 1911 to date

Until 1932 British-built Fords were assembled at Trafford Park, Manchester, and were Anglicized versions of the American Models T and A. However, with the building of the vast Dagenham factory, opened in 1932, Ford of Britain was able to produce models specifically designed for use in the U.K.

The first model to emerge from the new factory was the famous 933cc 8hp Model Y, with a simple sidevalve engine, three-speed gearbox and transverse leaf-spring suspension. The car, a full four-seater, was made in two- and four-door form, and the two-door model became the first full-sized saloon to be sold for £100, in late 1935. In the same year, the 1172cc 10hp Model C was introduced, an attractive car with flowing bodywork lines.

Above: 1935 10hp Model C saloon
Below: 1937 'New Eight' (7Y)

The Dagenham plant produced V8s based on American Fords, as well as a smaller 22hp '60' V8, produced from 1937 to 1939. The Model Y was replaced, in August 1937, by the 7Y, or 'New Eight', which featured more rounded styling, 'easy clean' disc wheels and doors hinged from the front – unusual in the 1930s. In the same year the Model C was replaced by the 10hp 7W, with similar bodywork modifications as for the 7Y.

The first Ford Anglia – the 8hp E04A –

Above: A 1940 8hp Anglia E04A

was introduced in November 1939, and produced again after the war until 1948. The Anglia was similar to the 7Y, but with a larger grille. The grille was changed again in 1946, when the new E494A Anglia now featured a narrow radiator cowl with a rounded top. The E494A was built until late 1953.

Above: Prefect E93A, 10hp, c. 1940
Below: 1948 Pilot V8 (3.6-litre)

The 10hp E93A, introduced in 1936, was the first Ford to be given the Prefect designation, and was identifiable by its protruding, rounded grille and rear-hinged 'alligator'-type bonnet. As with the Popular, production recommenced in 1945. The

car was altered in 1949, and redesignated E493A on receiving a grille with vertical bars and headlamps built into the front wings. In this form it continued until 1953.

It is interesting to note that the small van derivative of the Prefect – the E83W – was produced in large numbers throughout the war years. Indeed, some 350,000 were built for the forces.

From 1953 the Popular received the 1172cc sidevalve engine of the E493A Prefect to become a more austere version of the export 10hp Anglia. In this form (designated 103E) the Popular was the cheapest car on the U.K. market. The car was produced until August 1959 and as the last of the upright Fords was the last essentially pre-war design to be built in Britain.

Above: 1949 Anglia E494A

Above: 1950-56 Zephyr Mk I
Left: Ford's 'New' Anglia 100E of 1953
Below left: The four-door Prefect 100E

In the meantime, Ford had been updating its larger models, and the four-cylinder 1508cc Consul and the six-cylinder 2262cc Zephyr of 1951 had sleeker, unitary bodywork, and overhead-valve engines, albeit still mated to three-speed gearboxes. In 1954 a luxury variant – the Zephyr Zodiac – was introduced. Two-door convertible versions were available, in addition to the four-door saloons. Front suspension was by Mac-Pherson strut – a feature which was to stay with Ford into the 1980s.

At the 1953 Earls Court Motor Show Ford introduced its New Anglia (two-door) and New Prefect (four-door) models, with styling similar to that used on the larger cars. Both the new models were of unitary construction, and both featured a large luggage boot. While the engines were still of 1172cc capacity, they were more powerful, and totally redesigned compared with the earlier sidevalve units. Three-speed gearboxes were still fitted. Like the larger Fords, the new Anglia and Prefect models now had MacPherson-strut front suspension and hydraulic brakes.

New (Mark II) Consul, Zephyr and Zodiac models appeared in February 1956, with 'lowline' versions being introduced in February 1959. The Consul now had a 59bhp 1703cc engine, while the six-cylinder models had a capacity of 2553cc giving 85bhp.

One of Ford's most significant models – the 105E Anglia – was introduced in 1959. Unlike earlier Fords, it featured an over-square overhead-valve engine of 997cc capacity and a four-speed gearbox. The Anglia was later also fitted with a 1200cc engine (123E), and the model continued in production until 1967, selling very well for Ford, and earning it new respect. The 100E Anglia was updated and became the latest Popular, and was sold until 1962 – the last volume-production car in the UK to be fitted with a sidevalve engine. A few thousand (100E) Prefects were fitted with the 105E's overhead-valve engine, and termed 107E.

Above right: 1959 997cc ohv Anglia 105E
Right: 1962 2.6-litre Zodiac

Above: 1961-3 Consul Classic

Below: 1962 1200cc Consul Cortina

The four-door 1340cc (later 1498cc) Classic and the two-door fastback Capri version were introduced in 1961, but were only sold until 1963 (Classic) and 1964 (Capri). The large Mark III Zephyrs and Zodiacs, with angular, finned styling, were introduced in 1962, and used engines of identical capacities to the earlier models, but now linked to four-speed, all-synchromesh gearboxes.

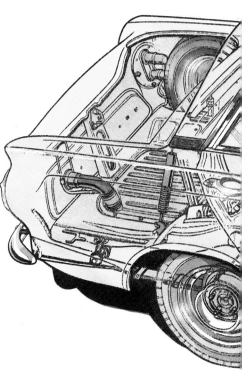

Above: Ford's mechanically 'traditional' Cortina was one of the most significant models in the history of the company. From the introduction of the Mk I in 1962,

Above: The sleek V4 Corsair, 1965

Above: 1964 Cortina Lotus in action

The most famous family Ford of all time – the Cortina – was introduced in 1962, and proved to be a winner for Ford in sales terms. Mark I models had 1200cc or 1500cc engines, based on that of the 105E Anglia. GT and Lotus versions were also built, the latter having a twin-cam 1558cc engine which produced 105bhp and 174km/h (108mph).

The more luxurious 1500cc Corsair was introduced in 1963, and was fitted with a V4 engine, initially of 1663cc but of 1996cc from 1965.

April 1966 saw the introduction of the huge Mark IV Zephyrs and Zodiacs. The Zephyr Four had a two-litre V4 engine, the Zephyr Six/Zodiac, a three-litre V6. A luxury 'Executive' version of the Zodiac was available from October 1966.

Restyled Mark II versions of the Cortina were introduced in late 1966, with a choice of 1.3-litre or 1.5-litre engines. From August 1967, the Cortinas featured 'cross-flow' Kent engines, in which the inlet and exhaust manifolds were on opposite sides of the unit. Again, a Cortina Lotus was available, from March 1967. Later that year a sports/luxury version of the Cortina – the 1600E – was introduced, fitted with a GT engine developing 88bhp. More than 1,010,000 Cortinas were sold in Mark I form, and virtually the same number of Mark IIs.

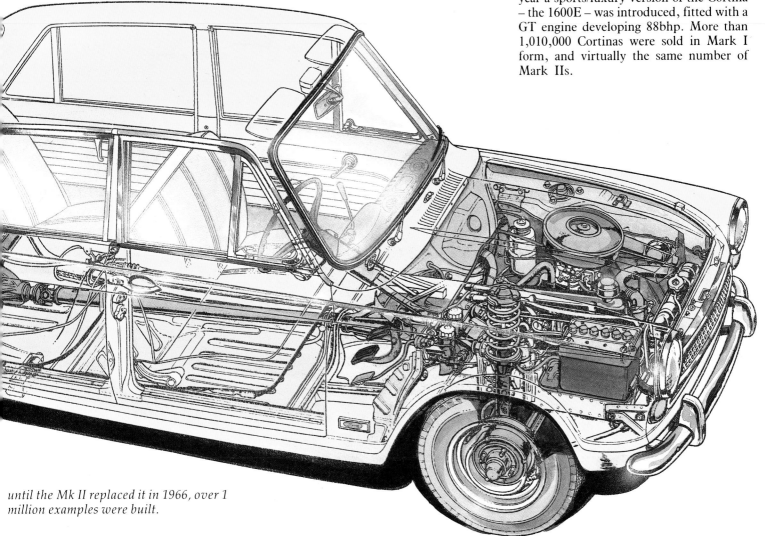

until the Mk II replaced it in 1966, over 1 million examples were built.

The Ford Anglia was replaced by the new Ford Escort at the end of 1967, the new car being available in 1.1, 1.3, 1.3GT and 1558cc Twin-Cam form, initially. Fast Mark I Escorts were to include, from January 1970, the BDA-engined twin-cam RS1600; from November 1970, the 1600cc Escort Mexico; from October 1971, the Escort Sport; and, from June 1973, the Pinto-powered RS2000. Ford's sporting image was also greatly enhanced by four victories at Le Mans in the late 1960s, regular international rallying successes in the 1970s, and 155 Grands Prix win for its Cosworth-built DFV engine between 1967 and 1983.

In January 1969, Ford introduced its sporting saloon – the Capri – at first in 1300, 1600 and 2000GT form. Three-litre V6-engined GTs were to follow.

Above: 1972 Mk III Cortina 1600XL   *Below: 1974 three-litre Capri Ghia*

The Cortina was updated and a Mark III version introduced in late 1970. The Cortinas employed overhead-camshaft 'Pinto' engines, in 1.6- and 2.0-litre versions, from 1973. A 2000E model was introduced in September 1973.

A new range of the large Consul and Granada models was introduced in 1972, using two-litre V4 or three-litre V6 engines. Series II Capris were introduced in March 1974, the new models featuring versatile hatchback bodywork.

Mark II versions of the Escort were announced in January 1975 with restyled bodywork. Sporting versions of the Mark II were later to include the RS1800, the

Left: 1976 Cortina 2000 Ghia

1600cc Mexico and the RS2000.

In July 1976 Ford produced its first small front-wheel-drive hatchback, the Fiesta, available in 957cc, 1116cc and 1298cc form, and with a wide range of trim levels. In September of the same year, a new-look Mark IV Cortina was introduced, with sleeker bodywork than the

Mark III.

Restyled Granadas were announced in August 1977, the engines now fitted being the two-litre overhead-camshaft Pinto unit, 2.3- or 2.8-litre V6s, or a 2.1-litre four-cylinder diesel made by Peugeot.

The Capri bodywork was made more aerodynamic from March 1978, and a 2.8-litre, fuel-injected V6 version was introduced in July 1981.

Increasingly, through the 1970s and 1980s, Ford's European production was spread between different centres, and factories were located in Spain, France, Belgium, Holland and Germany, as well as in Britain (notably Dagenham and Halewood).

The last Cortinas, the Mark V models, were introduced in September 1979 with a new grille and other minor changes.

Left: 1976 front-wheel-drive Fiesta
Above: Granada 2000 L, October 1977

Below: Ford Fiesta 1100S of the late 1970s

Below: Ford's front-wheel-drive Escort, introduced in 1980, gave hatchback versatility to their mid-range models. Like their predecessors, the new Escorts, available with a range of trim levels and engine sizes, were popular with buyers.

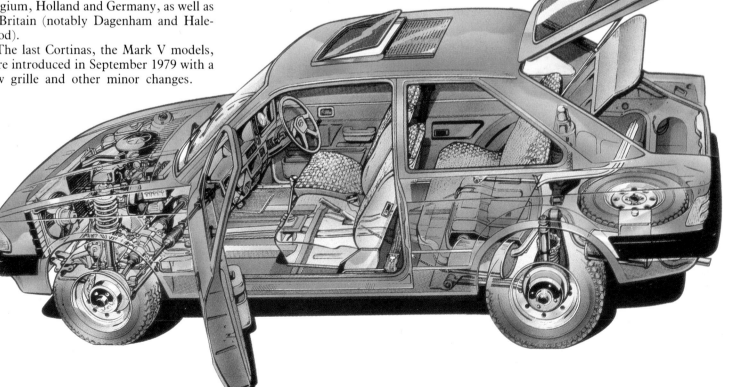

In September 1980 Ford introduced a new front-wheel-drive Escort hatchback, in three- and five-door form, with 1.1-, 1.3- or 1.6-litre engines. Sports versions designated XR3 and XR3i (fuel-injected) were also available.

The larger rear-wheel-drive Sierra hatchback was introduced as the replacement for the Cortina in October 1982 with a choice of overhead-camshaft engines of between 1.3- and 2.3-litres (the last a V6) and, later, with a 1.8-litre capacity. The fastest version, the racing-inspired Sierra RS Cosworth – with a 204bhp 2.0-litre turbocharged Pinto engine modified by Cosworth Engineering of Grand Prix fame – boasted a top speed of 241km/h (150mph) and a 0-60mph statistic of 6.7 seconds.

In 1983 a saloon version of the Escort – the Orion – became available, initially only with upmarket trim levels. From March 1986 the Escort range was updated and a 'lean-burn' overhead-camshaft 1.4-litre engine was introduced to the model.

The top-of-the-range Granadas continued throughout the 1980s, with a totally new hatchback range being announced in May 1985. The new cars were powered by overhead-camshaft four-cylinder engines of 1.8- or two-litres, a 2.8-litre V6, or a 2.5-litre diesel.

In January 1987 new 2.4-litre and 2.9-litre, overhead-camshaft four-cylinder

Above: 1982 Sierra hatchback

Below: The Sierra was the successor to the Cortina. It had hatchback bodywork, and, unlike most of its competitors of the time, retained rear-wheel-drive. Subtle changes were made to the body styling during the production life of the model.

Above: Capri S of the early 1980s
Left: 1987 Granada Scorpio hatchback
Below: The Fiesta range was updated in September 1983, when the styling was revised. Engine sizes ranged from 957cc to 1597cc (in the sporty XR2). Five-speed gearboxes were available with 1100cc and larger engines.

engines were introduced to the range, which was topped by the Scorpio 2.9i Executive model. Saloon versions of the Sierra – designated Sierra Sapphires – were introduced in February 1987.

The end of an era came in March 1987, when the last Capri – the 280 – was introduced, with special leather trim and based on the 2.8 Injection Special.

With the arrival of the 1990s, Ford unified its operations in Europe, with both British and German divisions making and selling the same ranges. In 1993, Ford Germany planned to cut 6,000 jobs to move the balance of power in Europe back to Britain.

Meanwhile, the Ford range was evolving steadily.

The Escort range was rejuvenated in 1990. The changes were evolutionary rather than revolutionary. Although the styling was brought up to date, the cars were still very recognizably related to their predecessors. The famous RS2000 name was brought back to life in 1991, replacing the XR3 tag. A year later the range received the all-new 16-valve Zetec engine, which was a big improvement on the crude engines previously used. Minor detail changes were made to the styling during the 1990s, with some face-lifts were more successful than others.

Ford's best-selling Fiesta was updated in 1989. New smoother styling and a five-door option helped boost sales. The pick of the Mk3 Fiestas was the RS Turbo, the first Fiesta with forced induction. Like the Escort, the Fiesta gained the Zetec engine but only in 1.8-litre guise. The smaller

Right: 1995 Fiesta Classic

Below: 1994 Ford Mondeo 24-valve V6

Top: For 1997, the U.S.-built Ford Explorer was offered to European buyers to compete with the Chrysler Cherokee and Grand Cherokee, already being imported to Europe

Above: The popular Mk4 Escort Cabriolet. This is the range-topping XR3i 16-valve model

Left: The RS2000 name was revived in 1991 for the new sporty Escort. It replaced the XR3i as the high-performance model in the Escort range. High insurance premiums made for slow sales

engines remained as before. A new Fiesta was launched in 1995 with a new range of engines. Mazda marketed the same car in Europe, as the 121.

The Sierra was replaced in 1993 by the new Mondeo. This attempt at a world car also sold in the States as the Contour. It was front-wheel-drive, unlike its predecessor, and, thanks to plenty of work by Ford engineers, the all-important NVH (noise, vibration and harshness) was kept to a minimum.

Above: Rather than design its own 4x4 to compete with Vauxhall's Frontera, Ford rebadged Nissan's Terrano as the Ford Maverick

Right: The Scorpio replaced the Granada in 1994. Its questionable styling did nothing to help the sales figures

The Mondeo was initially fitted only with four-cylinder engines but gained an all-new 2.5-litre V6 in 1994.

The old range-topper in Europe, the Granada, was replaced in 1994 by the Scorpio. This raised much comment in the press on account of its somewhat controversial styling and was often described as having been designed by committee.

In order to keep up with the current trend for MPVs, Ford, in collaboration with VW, created the Galaxy. The top-of-the-range model even used VW's VR6 engine. At the other end of the market, Ford placed a new car below the Fiesta. The Ka was very modern in its styling but used the Fiesta's old 1.3-litre engine. It was widely praised by the press but it took the buying public a little while to get used to the car's wacky looks.

The Puma was a new small coupé aimed squarely at Vauxhall's Tigra. Launched in 1997, it was dynamically a much better car than its rival. Other offerings in Europe were the Maverick, a rebadged Nissan Terrano 4x4, the American Probe coupé and the Explorer.

The Ford 2000 plan looked set to see much more commonality between European and American Ford cars by the turn of the century.

Above: Post-1996 face-lifted Mondeo estate

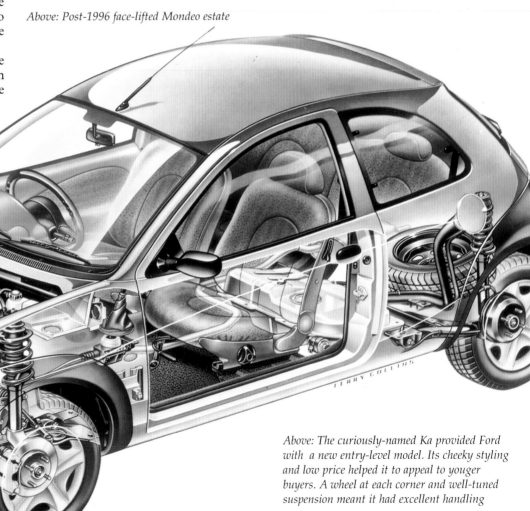

Above: The curiously-named Ka provided Ford with a new entry-level model. Its cheeky styling and low price helped it to appeal to youger buyers. A wheel at each corner and well-tuned suspension meant it had excellent handling

Right: The Ford Ka, was styled and priced to appeal to younger buyers

Below: The Ford Galaxy was the result of a joint project with Volkswagen

Bottom: The Ford Puma, launched in 1997, used a 1.7-litre 16-valve engine

Ford Australia 1925 to date

Although Ford cars were available in Australia from 1908, they were actually manufactured in Canada until 1925, when the Model T and Model A bodies became Australian produced – the latter still on American-made chassis. Production was initially based in Geelong, Victoria, later with assembly plants in Granville, Brisbane, Adelaide and Fremantle. This was under the supervision of a Canadian team lead by H. C. French.

Unfortunately, the Model T was at the end of its popularity by this time and Ford was considerably behind its main rival, General Motors, for sales. The Ford V8s, which arrived in 1932, were more what the car-buying public wanted, but proved too expensive.

From 1934 onwards Australian Fords began to develop their own personality having been hitherto almost identical to the Canadian range except for a slight alteration in roof line on the Tudor sedans. Most noted of the new vehicles was the closed-cabin pickup or 'utility vehicle', a style subsequently widely copied by other manufacturers.

French retired in 1950 and was replaced by C. A. Smith, who increased the Australian-made content of the cars to over 90 per cent. Ten years later a new plant at Broadmeadows was opened for production of the six-cylinder Falcon, aimed directly at the successful Holden. The Falcon gained a V8 engine in 1966, and was joined on the market by the V8 Fairlane the following year.

The distinctive styling of these two cars was continued in the Fairmont, Fairlane and LTD V8s, separating them from the American Fords of the same name. In the 1980s the range also included smaller, Mazda-based vehicles like the Laser, Telstar and two-seater Capri convertible. Ford finally achieved its long-held ambition to take over as market leader from Holden in 1982.

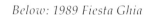

Above: 1989 Orion GL   *Below: 1989 Fiesta Ghia*

Franklin

U.S.A.
1902–1934

Herbert H. Franklin was a specialist in the production of diecastings, forming his own company, the H. H. Franklin Manufacturing Co. in Syracuse, New York, in 1895. In 1901 he was introduced to John Wilkinson's air-cooled car prototypes by transmission manufacturers A. T. Brown and C. A. Lipe. Franklin ordered a Wilkinson-designed vehicle, and the following year the first Franklin car went on sale.

Franklin was to continue with air-cooled power units throughout the company's existence, and also used laminated wooden-frame chassis up until 1928.

In 1905 the first six-cylinder car was launched and Franklin tried an unsuccessful competition straight-eight. Recirculating full-pressure lubrication appeared on the 1912 models, which had Renault-style front bodywork. Four-cylinder engines were dropped in 1913, and the following year left-hand drive was standardized.

The Franklin Automobile Co. was formed in 1917. Various other firms tried to imitate the company's success, with

Above: 1929 air-cooled Franklin Six; the radiator is false
Below: 1909 Franklin Torpedo displays typically unconventional styling

10,000 cars a year sold throughout the 1920s. Bodywork by J. F. de Causse, attempting to conventionalize the new Series II's appearance by adding a false radiator, led to Wilkinson's resignation. Custom coachwork was also available by Derham, Willoughby, Holbrook and Dietrich.

Franklin's first front-wheel brakes came on the Airman series of 1928, so-named because of famous owners Charles Lindbergh and Amelia Earhart, and latching onto air-cooled aero-engine fame. Because of their comparatively light weight, Franklins were used to power aircraft during this period.

Sales plummeted in the Depression, despite worldwide exports, and management appointed by the bank cheapened the range to cut costs. The last model was the Olympic, using Reo bodywork, and the factory closed in 1934. The Franklin name was acquired by former engineers Edward Marks and Carl Dorman and a water-cooled version of the air-cooled engine was used in the 1947 Tucker.

Frazer-Nash

Great Britain 1924–1957

Archie Frazer-Nash formed Frazer-Nash Ltd. in November 1922 and his first cars were modified chain-drive vehicles bought from his former employer G.N. Ltd.

The first Frazer-Nash proper was built at the Kingston, Surrey, factory and announced in 1924. It had a 1½-litre overhead-valve Plus Power engine and then Anzani power units.

Frazer-Nash merged with William G. Thomas, converters of ex-War Department lorries, in October 1925 and the new company was known as William G. Thomas and Frazer-Nash Ltd.

The merger had lasted two years when Richard Plunkett-Greene stepped in with several thousand pounds. Frazer-Nash himself became seriously ill in 1928 and the company – now known as A.F.N. Ltd. – passed to H. J. Aldington who had been with Frazer-Nash since its earliest days.

With his brother, Bill, he went on to control Frazer-Nash until the company closed.

The Frazer-Nash changed little in 15 years. And although it was relatively crude, with chains and dog-clutches in its transmission, its following remained small but loyal.

Production remained modest with fewer than 50 cars leaving the premises in any year and the factory moved to new premises in Isleworth, Middlesex, in 1930.

Aldington collaborated with B.M.W. to produce the Frazer-Nash-B.M.W. and models sold in England included the Type 34 (B.M.W. 315), Type 40 (B.M.W. 315 or 319) and the Type 55 (315 Sports).

Sales of the chain-driven cars dropped from 1935 onwards and only one was sold in 1939. But more than 700 Frazer-Nash-B.M.W.s were sold between December 1934 and September 1939.

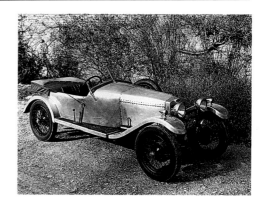

Above: 1925 Frazer-Nash Fast Tourer

Below: c. 1924 Frazer-Nash tourer

Below: Although Frazer-Nash continued to build cars like this 1934 T.T. Replica, the main source of the company's income in the '30s was the B.M.W. collaboration

The Aldington brothers served in the army during World War II, H. J. becoming involved with the Bristol Aeroplane Company.

As a result, Frazer-Nash built sports models with Bristol engines and gearboxes and, of the variety of models offered, the Le Mans replica was the most successful in competition and sales.

The last new model was the Continental coupé with a 3.2-litre B.M.W. V8 engine. It was launched in 1956 and priced at £3,751 – not competitive with the £3,076 Aston Martin DB2/4 and £1,711 Jaguar XK140 coupé.

Only two Continentals were made, the last in 1957.

A.F.N. continues to flourish as one of the U.K.'s major Porsche concessionaires.

Right: Frazer-Nash Sebring and A.F.N. staff. (L-R) Nelson Ledger, W.H. Aldington, George Sneath, H.J. Aldington, Harry Olrog

Left: Frazer-Nash T.T. Replica, built in 1935
Below left: Frazer-Nash B.M.W. Type 55, built in 1939, shortly before the outbreak of the Second World War
Below: The highly successful 1951 Frazer-Nash Le Mans Replica

FSO

Poland
1946 to date

Fabryka Samochodow Osbowych, or FSO, was set up as a state-owned company in 1946. Also known as Polski-Fiat the company started business by manufacturing the two-stroke Russian Gaz Pobieda and selling it as the Warszawa, mainly on the Polish market.

The state-owned company renewed an agreement with Fiat in 1968 and began to build the FSO 125P. The 125P used old Fiat 1300/1500 running gear and engines with newer 124 bodywork. The car lasted until 1991, by which time it was very out of date and competed with the Russian Ladas which were also an old Fiat design. Not even bargain basement pricing could disguise the grinding engines and crude suspension.

With no alternative to the aged Fiat running gear, FSO engineers set about designing its own hatchback on the 125P floorpan. The new car was called the Polonez and was launched in 1975. The narrow track looked out of place under the bulky body, but it was a brave effort given the

Above: The Caro was an updated version of the Polonez, introduced in the early 1990s, in an effort to increase sales

Below: The Polonez was FSO's first hatchback but someone forgot to tell the designers that hatchbacks should have a folding rear seat

Above: Until the 1990s, FSO had used the same Fiat pushrod engines dating from the 1950s
Right: Interiors were improved for the Caro, but it still looked ten years out of date when new
Below: As a cheap working vehicle, the Caro pick-up is in its element

ingredients. Unfortunately, someone forgot to tell the design team that a hatchback is meant to have a folding rear seat – the omission was corrected on later models.

Rock bottom pricing could not prevent FSO's decline during the early 1990s. Plunging depreciation spelled the end, before an unexpected revival in 1993 under new management.

The Polonez was updated in the early-1990s with mildly softened lines, but still with same ancient mechanicals. Now called the Caro, the car gained a Peugeot diesel engine in 1992 and even a 16-valve unit in the shape of Rover's excellent 1.4-litre, 103 horsepower K-series engine. With the latter, a brave driver could take the Caro to 100mph (160km/h). The new car was certainly a more saleable product, especially with such a low asking price and sold well enough to keep the company afloat.

GAZ

U.S.S.R.
1932 to date

GAZ, the Gorkovsky Avtomobilni Zavod or Gorky Automobile Works, was set up in 1932 at Gorky in what was then heralded as the biggest vehicle manufacturing plant in Europe. It was certainly the first major car factory in the U.S.S.R. and relied initially on assistance from Ford U.S.A. with designs for the factory buildings, machine-tools and components.

Trucks preceded cars as a priority, and both commercial and civilian models bore a close resemblance to their Ford counterparts. Not surprisingly, production runs were far longer, however, and the GAZ-A cars continued to be made until 1936, with truck versions not being replaced until 1948. Again, the A-model's successor, the M-1, was stylistically like an earlier Ford saloon, and its replacement in 1940 bore no real external evidence of stylistic progression. The engines were different, however, rising from 3.2-litre four-cylinder units to 3.4-litre straight-sixes.

Production was largely given over to building 4×4 utilities during World War II, together with trucks and a few 4×4 11-40 and 11-73 saloons.

GAZ emerged from the hostilities with a brand-new saloon, the Andrei Lipgart-designed M-20 Pobieda, or Victory, which looked not unlike the contemporary Standard Vanguard, and which remained in production until 1958. The M-20 was powered by a 2.1-litre four-cylinder engine, and of the 237,172 cars built, a number were 4×4s and convertibles. The same model was manufactured in Poland as the Warszawa, eventually using entirely Polish-sourced components; here it lasted until 1972, with about 253,000 having been made.

Alongside the M-20 was the larger 3.5-litre six-cylinder GAZ M-12 or Z1M, also designed by Lipgart, and which was made between 1951 and 1960. This car was not generally available to the public, although 21,546 units were produced, some going for export to Finland and Sweden.

From 1959, the intermediate Soviet official or professional was catered for by the Chaika, or Seagull, now fitted with 5.5-litre V8 engines. Top people rode around in the Z1S or Z1L limousines. There was a 12-year hiatus in Chaika production between 1965 and 1977, at which later date the model reappeared with the same engine but updated styling.

The M-20 Pobieda's successor was the 2.5-litre 70bhp Volga, introduced in 1955, and which, with face-lifts in 1968 and 1982, was until the mid-1980s the most numerous medium-sized car in the Soviet Union.

The Volga 3102 was widely exported, and was available with either the 2.5-litre petrol or two- and 2.2-litre Indenor diesel engines. Given the freer economic climate of the Gorbachev era, with its emphasis on profits, there will be greater efforts to market the ZAZ 1102, a 1.1-litre three-door front-wheel-drive model, developed over a six-year period and launched in 1988.

Above: 1932 Ford Model T-based GAZ-A

Below: 1940 GAZ-11-73
Bottom: 1969 Volga M.24, 2455cc,
145km/h (90mph) saloon

G.N.

Great Britain 1910-1925

H. R. Godfrey and Captain Archibald Frazer-Nash, whose surnames combined into G.N. Ltd., began business in the stables of the latter's home in Hendon, north London, where the first half-dozen or so of their cyclecars were produced.

They presented their first vehicle to the public in 1910, powered by a J.A.P. or Peugeot engine. The G.N. was one of a number of cars which brought economy motoring to large sections of the population who would previously have used a motor cycle and sidecar combination.

From 1911 Godfrey and Frazer-Nash began offering engines of their own manufacture, although built with some Peugeot parts, and until the outbreak of World War I various forms of belt and chain drive were used.

After the war, the British arm of Grégoire bought the company, which then became G.N. Motors Ltd., moving the following year to new premises at East Hill, Wandsworth, London. Extra staff were taken on, production of the aptly-named Popular model and its variants dramatically increased, and the firm even employed mobile engineers to service cus-

tomers' vehicles. Overseas, G.N. cyclecars were produced under licence by the French Salmson company between 1919 and 1922.

By 1921 the advent of the light car was eclipsing cyclecars, and falling sales led to the receivers being called in to take control of future production. The following year both the founders left after arguments over the type of vehicles to be made. Godfrey set up a G.N. servicing company and was later to form H.R.G. with E. A. Halford and Guy H. Robins. He died in 1968. Frazer-Nash founded his own famous marque from small beginnings with left-over G.N. parts in 1922.

Now making a loss, G.N. Motors Ltd. was wound up in 1923. The following year two former employees, having formed G.N. Ltd., brought out an Anzani-powered model, but by 1925 the marque had disappeared.

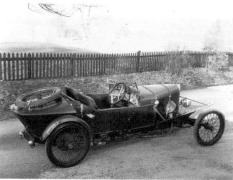

Right: A GN special named 'Spider' hillclimbed between the wars
Below: Reproductions of early 1920s racers

Top: A distinctive 1914 tourer
Centre: 1921 French-built GN
Above: A 1922 GN survivor

Gobron-Brillié

France
1898–1930

Although the marque was officially named Gobron-Brillié until 1919, Eugene Brillié split from Gustave Gobron in 1903, after only five years of partnership. It was he who designed their famous 'vibrationless' engine produced until 1922.

They formed the Société des Moteurs Gobron-Brillié in 1898 with premises in Paris, moving to Boulogne-sur-Seine two years later. The cars were sold in Britain as Teras and were also produced under licence in Belgium by Nagant.

The early model was doubtfully claimed to run on gin, whisky and brandy as well as petrol, and was recorded as running on alcohol in the 1902 Concours du Ministre. Indeed, the Nancéienne company won the 1901 Paris–Roubaix race for alcohol-fuelled cars with a Gobron-Brillié-designed vehicle produced under patent.

By 1903 all models were front-engined and the company had begun some forays into motor sport. The following year their 13½-litre racer officially broke the 160km/h (100mph) barrier, although its subsequent entries in the 1904/5 Gordon Bennett Eliminating Trials and the 1906/7 Grands Prix proved disappointing.

Up until World War I the company produced a variety of vehicles, including an unlikely 70/90hp six-cylinder machine. The models had a mixture of shaft and chain drive, the latter being continued as late as 1914.

After the war Gobron-Brillié moved to Levallois-Perret and became Automobiles Gobron. Sales were fairly low for the remainder of the firm's existence, despite attempts to market the cars by the Stabilia company under its own name. The rather splendid 25CV of 1922 gave way to a conventional Chapuis-Dornier-engined car, also unsuccessful.

Gobron made a final try with its super-charged Turbo-Sport model of 1928, but a very limited number were produced, and the company folded in 1930.

Above: The 15-20hp Gobron Berline
Below: A 1906 40/60hp model

The 1904 racer with its immense 13½-litre engine broke the 160km/h (100mph) barrier and featured mechanically-operated sidevalves on its four cylinders. However, it did not achieve much in the way of sporting success thereafter.

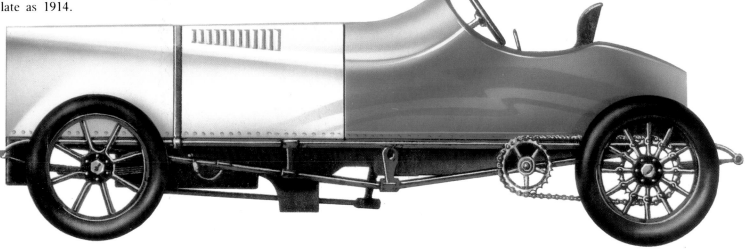

Graham-Paige
U.S.A.
1927–1940

Graham-Paige may appear to be just another fairly obscure American marque which lasted less than 20 years and produced only a few notable models. But indirectly it gave a leg up to one of the present day's largest volume-car producers and the company itself lives on today in a most unusual way.

In 1927 three brothers from Indiana, Robert, Joseph and Ray Graham, took over the Paige-Detroit Motor Company, a fairly successful firm which had made quite a name for itself since it started in 1908 with cars like the 1921 Daytona Speedster, named after a 102mph (164km/h) record-breaking run by one of its models.

The brothers themselves had made their money from agriculture, bottle-making, and assembling trucks with their own bodies on Dodge chassis and engines; a business which Dodge bought from them in 1925.

As soon as they bought the Paige concern, and its factory in Dearborn, Michigan, the three renamed it Graham-Paige and started to employ their business and salesmanship skills to good effect. They established a first-year sales record with their 1928 range, which was cannily priced and targeted within the market, and in 1929 they made nearly 80,000 cars and had to take over several more plants to cope with the demand – even opening one in Berlin.

But this phenomenal success was not to last – indeed, 1929 was to prove their best-ever year. The Depression began to affect sales badly, and the firm only just weathered the economic storm of the early 1930s which claimed so many small companies.

In 1932 it bounced back, now known simply as Graham, with its Blue Streak models, which were low (thanks to a clever chassis design), sleek, and extremely stylish. Though the cars were widely admired, they weren't as widely bought, and sales continued to slide. Even the excellent

performance of the range, improved further when a supercharged model appeared in 1934, could not help to stop their fall, and the only bright spot was the sale of tools and dies for an obsolete model to Nissan of Japan, thereby temporarily saving the company and starting Nissan's rise to its present position as one of the world's biggest volume-car makers.

But nothing, it seemed, could halt the company's demise. The 1938 'Sharknose' range was a brave, if phenomenally ugly, attempt to gain attention and though they performed well, they looked like the result of a nasty crease in the blueprints and didn't sell. Floundering badly by now, the last model built, in 1940, was a mixture of Cord, Hupmobile and Graham parts which met the fate it deserved – ignominious failure.

The company stopped making cars entirely in 1940, though World War II led it briefly into aircraft and marine engines, not to mention an amphibious tractor. After the war the car-making part of the firm was absorbed into the Kaiser-Frazer corporation.

Graham made farm machinery for a while, then became involved in real estate and survives today, in spirit if not in name, as the corporation which owns and runs the giant Madison Square Gardens sporting arena.

Below: A 1939 Graham-Paige chassis with Amherst Villers body

Bottom: The 1941 Graham Hollywood

Grégoire

France
1942–1970

When Jean Albert Grégoire began the Grégoire firm in 1942, his was the second French marque to use that name, the first being in the Seine-et-Oise district of Paris between 1903 and 1924. The French designer began work on his first Grégoire model during World War II, and a running prototype was assembled by 1942.

Grégoire had already gained a great deal of experience as a manufacturer of cars. From 1926 to 1934 he had been responsible for proving the worth of front-wheel drive, both for road and competition use, with his sporting Tracta designs. After Tracta, Grégoire had worked for Amilcar, which was then under Hotchkiss control, launching the technically unusual and lightweight Compound car with all-round independent suspension. This made use of an aluminium or light-alloy casting for the chassis and unit construction. It also incorporated front-wheel drive – as did most of his vehicles – from J. A. Grégoire Tracta patents.

Grégoire's first design, built by l'Aluminium Français, was known as the Aluminium Français Grégoire, or A.F.G. It was turned down by major French manufacturers Peugeot, Simca, Citroën and Renault, but sold by Panhard as the Panhard Dyna. A few were built in England by Member of Parliament Denis Kendall under that name, and a licence

was gained by Australian Lawrence Hartnett, but little came of either venture.

In the early 1950s Grégoire designed a four-cylinder car which was produced as a joint venture with Hotchkiss, and was continued briefly after that company folded. In 1956 Grégoire tried again, this time with a supercharged model designed by Henri Chapron, and made in limited numbers until 1962 in the old Tracta factory at Asnières.

Heavy losses were incurred, however, and it was not until 1970 that Grégoire tried again, with an electric-powered prototype, but this never went into production.

Top: Grégoire's first design, sold by Panhard as the Panhard Dyna c. 1946
Above: The Socéma-Grégoire turbine car of 1954
Left: 2.2-litre convertible of 1959, one of only ten ever made

Hampton

Great Britain
1912–1931

The Hampton Engineering Company began building cars in 1912. The first model was a 1.7-litre four-cylinder 12/16, assembled using components from abroad.

Prior to World War I, a twin-cylinder, two-stroke light car was produced, followed by an 8hp cyclecar. Then came another lightweight car, powered by a 1.2-litre engine.

After the war, the firm moved from Birmingham to near Stroud, in Gloucestershire, and produced an overhead-valve 1½-litre 10/16, the new model again following established light-car chassis design.

In 1920 a 1.8-litre variant was introduced; both cars had Dorman engines, driving through gearboxes of Hampton's own manufacture.

The company was restructured in 1920, after which it had considerable success in motor sport and hill-climbs. A Hampton lapped Brooklands at around 90mph (145km/h).

Meadows engines – in 1.8- and 1.2-litre (Junior) capacities – were fitted from 1923, and the following year a 2.1-litre model became available, plus a new 1½-litre 12hp Hampton.

The company then suffered more financial problems and another restructuring, following which its 12hp model was revised.

In 1927 the company added a 1.7-litre six-cylinder 15/45 to its range, and in 1928 a 9hp model, with the mechanical components of the Junior fitted to new bodywork.

In 1929 a three-litre, 20hp model was offered with an overhead-valve six-cylinder engine.

Hampton incorporated some ingenious technical developments in its cars of the late 1920s and early 1930s. For example, adjustable rear suspension was available on its 12/40 model. The firm also worked on the Cowburn gearbox, which used coned rollers and coil springs instead of conventional gears.

By 1931 the company was facing ruinous financial problems. The last Hamptons included another 12hp model (1.2-litres), 2.2-litre straight-eights, 18hp cars with Röhr engines, and a 2.4-litre model with a six-cylinder sidevalve engine.

Top: A Hampton 14hp, c. 1926, near Stroud
Right: 1928 Hampton 12/40
Below: 1924 all-weather Hampton Junior

Healey

Great Britain 1946–1954

Donald Healey was a well-known figure in British motor sport in the 1930s, and he turned his hand to car manufacture in 1946 after working for both Riley and Triumph. The 1946 Healey used a modified 2.4-litre Riley engine and other Riley running components in a new chassis which had excellent roadholding properties.

Healeys were offered either as bare chassis or with lightweight aerodynamic two-door saloon bodywork by Elliot or convertible bodywork by Westland. These were very potent machines indeed, and one achieved a maximum speed of 111.87mph (180.03km/h) in Belgium to substantiate Healey's claim to make the fastest production car in the world. The make soon became very successful in competitive events at home and abroad.

The original models were supplemented by a rather square-rigged Sportsmobile drophead coupé in 1948, but this lasted only until 1950. In that year, the Elliot and Westland models were replaced by a Tickford-bodied saloon and an Abbott-bodied drophead. In addition, there was a lightweight two-seater model called the Silverstone, which was little short of a road-going racing car. Fearing that supplies of the Riley engine would soon dry up, Healey sought alternatives and found both the three-litre Alvis engine and the 3.8-litre Nash engine, each of which he put into new models. During 1951, he drew up plans for yet another model, with which he intended to exploit the North American sports-car market. This time, he used an Austin engine. This design was taken up by Austin's Leonard Lord as a new Austin-built car and renamed the Austin-Healey (q.v.). The last Healey, a Nash-engined car, was made in 1954.

Top: 1949 Healey Sportsmobile
Above centre: Nash Healey of 1952
Below centre: 1946-50 Healey Westland
Right: A distinctive Healey Tickford
Far right: 1950 Healey Silverstone

Hillman

Great Britain
1907–1978

William Hillman founded the Hillman Motor Car Company in 1907, in which year he produced a 25hp four-cylinder car with Louis Coatelen, to take part in the Tourist Trophy race.

From the early days Hillman built family cars, introducing a 1357cc monobloc-engined 9hp model in 1912. The company's 10hp model of 1919 had a 1593cc sidevalve engine, later reduced to 1496cc and developing 18bhp (28bhp in the sporting version).

Hillman also built bigger cars in small numbers prior to World War I, including models with two-cylinder 1.8-litre engines, four-cylinder 6.4-litre units, and six-cylinder engines of two- and 9.7-litres capacity.

The 9hp Hillman continued in production, being regularly updated, until 1925; by then the engine had grown to 1.6 litres.

Above: M. Louis Coatelen and 1907 Hillman
Left: 1931 prototype Hillman Minx

Between 1926 and 1928 Hillman built only the Fourteen, which had a sidevalve engine and a four-speed gearbox. 'Safety' versions of the car, from 1929, had toughened glass and servo-assisted brakes. A larger model of the time had a 2.6-litre straight-eight engine.

The Hillman Imp of 1963 was an innovative small car, lively and economical. The two-door, four-seater featured a rear-mounted, 875cc overhead camshaft engine, driving the rear wheels.

In 1928 the Rootes brothers bought a controlling interest in Humber, which company in turn purchased Hillman. From 1932 both firms became an integral part of the Rootes Group. In the same year the first Hillman Minx – a 10hp 1185cc family saloon – was introduced. The Minx was extremely successful and offered a freewheel and radio in 1934 (the 'Melody' Minx) and all-synchromesh gear changing in 1935.

A sports version (the 'Aero' Minx) was also sold from 1933 and this car was developed into the Talbot/Sunbeam-Talbot Tens. Hillman also built larger models in the late 1930s, including a 14hp model with hydraulic brakes.

The 1940 model Minx was continued after the war, with chassisless unitary-construction bodywork. The 1949 Minx was given lower and wider bodywork, and the engine was enlarged to 1265cc in 1950.

Hillman produced a range of models, but from 1952 the firm concentrated on a new Minx, totally restyled to celebrate the 21st anniversary of the Minx. The new car had a 1265cc engine developing 38bhp. The car was initially available in saloon, estate and convertible forms and, from 1953, a Thrupp and Maberly-bodied Californian Hardtop was available. This coupé model had a large, wrap-around rear screen, slim door pillars and only two doors.

From 1955 a new grille was fitted, and 43bhp overhead-valve engines of 1390cc were fitted to the de luxe Minx. However, the models remained essentially the same until May 1956, when a completely new Minx was announced, with badge-engineered versions being available under the Singer Gazelle (luxury version) and Sunbeam Rapier (sporting derivative) names. The power output was now 51bhp. Two-door estate versions of the Minx were designated Husky.

The Jubilee Minx of 1957 was available with two-pedal Manumatic control, while in 1960 Easidrive automatic transmission was introduced. The engine was enlarged to 1490cc for 1959 models and to 1592cc for 1962, in which year the larger-bodied Super Minx was introduced.

In 1963 the revolutionary rear-engined Imp became available. This small car, built at Linwood, Glasgow, featured an all-alloy, overhead-camshaft 875cc engine

developing 39bhp, and all-round independent suspension.

A five-bearing 1725cc engine was fitted to the Minx and Super Minx in 1965, and an entirely new body shell was introduced for the Minx in 1967.

The 80bhp, 1725cc Hunter saloon ('Arrow') range replaced the Super Minx from 1957. A twin-carburettor GT version was available from October 1969.

The totally new Avenger saloon and estate-car range was introduced in February 1970, with adventurous styling and a choice of either 1248cc or 1498cc engines. High-performance GT versions were also produced. From 1973 a 1598cc engine was optional.

In September 1976 the Hillman name disappeared as the Chrysler (U.K.) organization took over the entire range.

Top left: 1927 14hp Hillman
Top right: Hillmans for Australia, 1951

Above left: 1955 Hillman Minx Mk VIII
Above: 1958 1390cc Hillman Husky

Left: 1963 Hillman Imp
Below left: 1973 Hillman Avenger GLS
Below: 1975 Hunter Topaz/Imp Caledonian

Hispano-Suiza
Spain
1904–1944

Over nearly four decades Hispano-Suiza produced a large range of high-quality cars with engines ranging in size from 3.6 to 11.3 litres, but four models stand out from the rest. These were the lightweight 3.6-litre Alfonso of 1912, the technically advanced 6.5-litre H6 of 1919, the powerful 8-litre 1924 Boulogne and the magnificent 1931 9.4-litre V12 Type 68.

Two men who were associated with the company almost from its inception were the Swiss engineer Marc Birkigt and the Spanish financier and company director Damien Mateu, who together developed a

Below: King Alfonso and his 1908 model

Top: A 1913 'Alfonso', named after the King of Spain
Above: A 1925 H6B bodied by Kellner

company which was innovative yet financially successful.

Birkigt was born in Geneva in 1878, qualified as a first-class mechanical engineer and undertook his obligatory military service in the artillery where he began to develop a lifelong interest in armaments. In 1900 he joined an engineering company in Barcelona and designed and built a small 4½hp car, before the failing company was taken over in June 1904 by Damien Mateu. The new organization was renamed 'Fabrica La Hispano-Suiza de Automobiles' indicating an amalgam of Spanish finance and leadership with Swiss engineering expertise.

A racing Hispano won the 1910 Coupe de l'Auto and from it was developed the famous 3.6-litre Alfonso, named in honour of the young King Alfonso XIII of Spain who owned some 30 Hispanos and was a long-standing patron of the company. At around this time Hispano opened a factory in Paris to assemble the Alfonso and a range of heavy luxury carriages for the more lucrative French market.

The Alfonso was probably the first true sports car, having been designed for both competiton and road use, and it came with a four-cylinder in-line 3.6-litre 64bhp engine, a three-speed (later four-speed) manual gearbox and a live rear axle. In a car weighing only 762kg (1680lb) the power-to-weight ratio was good. Another interesting feature was the very powerful gas headlights, designed and built by

The H6B of 1930 was essentially the same car that had been introduced in 1919 – a tribute to the quality of design that engineer Marc Birkigt had applied to both engine and chassis.

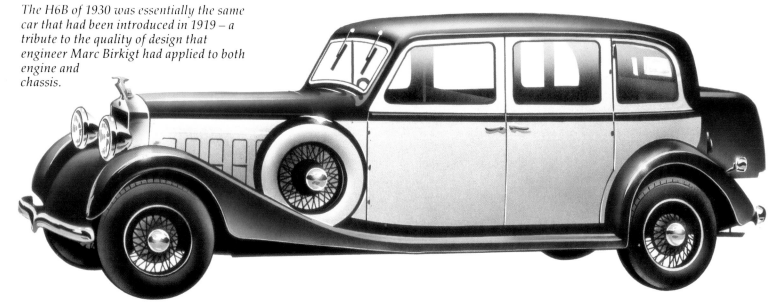

Blériot, the Channel aviator and manufacturer of lamps for lighthouses.

The Barcelona factory produced some rather mundane cars and commercial vehicles, while the French Hispano cars became rather more exotic, culminating in the immortal H6 (and 6B) of 1919 with its 6.5-litre 130bhp overhead-camshaft light-alloy engine and its seven-bearing pressure-lubricated camshaft. The long-stroke engine developed plenty of low-speed torque allowing the car to be driven from 16km/h to 138km/h (10mph to 86mph) in top gear. It was highly praised by the press and remained in production without major alterations until 1934.

Although not designed with competition in mind, the H6 did quite well in road-races, winning twice at Boulogne and finishing sixth in the 1924 Targa Florio. By this time a new eight-litre engine had been installed and production cars carried the name 'Boulogne' in recognition of their racing success.

Hispano-Suiza's last great fling, despite the Depression, was the production of the Type 68 (54/220CV in France) for the 1931 Paris Salon. This was the company's biggest, most complex and most expensive car to date, and although it arrived at a time of world economic depression, the huge 9.4-litre (or 11.3-litre in the Type 68 bis) V12-engined luxury saloon attracted many buyers and remained in production until Birkigt stopped manufacturing cars in 1938 to concentrate on his aircraft engines and armaments.

The Paris factory never fully recovered after World War II, and Birkigt, the quiet engineer, died peacefully in his native Switzerland in 1953.

Bodies by famous coachbuilders, like this coupé by Guiet, were the rule rather than the exception for Hispano-Suiza's moneyed clientele. This car shows off the stork mascot of the marque which commemorates French flying ace Georges Guynemer, a friend of Birkigt's killed in action during World War I.

Above: Fernandes et Darvin-bodied K6

Above: The 1927 'Barcelona'

Above: 1931's Type 68 with a V12 engine

Holden

Australia 1948 to date

Holden began as Holden and Frost in Adelaide, making coachwork for horse-drawn carriages and bodying its first car – a Lancia – in 1914. The company became Holden's Motor Body Builders Ltd. in 1920, and its work appeared on imported Morris vehicles during the following decade.

In 1931 Holden was bought by General Motors (Australia) Pty. Ltd. Subsequently, the bulk of its work was assembling British and American General Motors cars for the Australian market. In particular, this included Chevrolets and Buicks, although other makes such as Hudson, Essex, Chrysler, Plymouth, Willys, Reo and Studebaker were also provided with coachwork by Holden. The first Holden closed body appeared on an Essex in 1924.

In 1934 Sir Lawrence Hartnett became Managing Director of Holden and the company's first two-door fastback coupé

Above: 1934 coupé, just before the fastback style was introduced
Right: Holden 1937 roadster

was offered in 1938, several years before similar cars appeared on the American market. This distinctive style, built on a variety of different chassis, was known as the Sloper. It was to become Holden's trademark in the early years after World War II.

This 1967 Premier is already well known in several other guises to Europeans; many Vauxhall and Opel products ended up restyled slightly and re-badged as Holdens for the Australian market.

During the war Holden had produced military vehicles on the Canadian Military Pattern Chevrolet chassis, similar to those produced by Ford. After the war Hartnett gained the backing of the Australian government to build a new and entirely Australian car to fill the gap between the big American models and the much smaller British ones. Hartnett wanted this vehicle, a four-door sedan, to be of advanced design but General Motors vetoed the idea in favour of more-established construction and he resigned in 1947, the year before the new FX was launched.

The FX was immediately successful, and was joined by a coupé utility in 1951. Although Holden had continued to build bodies on imported chassis, the rise in price of these after the war made this an uneconomic proposition.

In May 1953 the FX was updated slightly into the FJ215, with more major changes coming with the FE of 1956. In 1954 Holden began exporting to New Zealand, and by the end of the 1950s it was building nearly half the private cars sold in Australia, leading the market until Ford took over as recently as 1982.

By 1967 the Torana had appeared, as well as larger V8-engined cars like the HK Belmont and Kingswood. Two years later the Chevrolet-engined Monaro coupé was introduced, giving Holden sporting success, and also the luxury American limousine-style Brougham. In the mid-1970s appeared the Isuzu-based Gemini, ending the idea of an entirely Australian car begun by Hartnett.

Continuing this trend was the best-selling Commodore, launched in 1979 with a variety of different engine sizes and inspired by European Vauxhall-Opel cars. The Brougham was replaced by the Statesman series, some of which were exported without engines for the Japanese market, and there fitted with Mazda rotary engines. Holden also provided Opel power units for the Swedish market since that country's emission regulations were almost identical to those of Australia, although the company never really exported to countries where General Motors already traded strongly.

More recently, Holden has marketed Japanese imports such as the Barina and the Astra which latter, although assembled

Above: The 48-215, c. 1954

Below: The 1948 model J in the outback

Above: 1955, start of an export boom

in Australia, was in essence the 1.5-litre Nissan Cherry. Nissan engines were also used in other Holden models.

Besides its original plant at Woodville, which continued to supply bodies, Holden also built a body plant in Elizabeth, South Australia, and one at Acacia Ridge, Queensland, as well as its main base at Fisherman's Bend. The company ran its assembly operations at Pagewood, New South Wales; The Valley, Brisbane; Mosman Park in Perth; and Birkenhead, South Australia, employing in total over 18,000 people. In addition, it has a factory for assembly at Upper Hutt, Wellington, New Zealand.

Below: The Gemini SL coupé of 1976

Towards the end of the 1980s, Holden launched a new range of cars that was to become the mainstay of the company for the 1990s. The Holden VS models were all based on the old Opel Senator. Unlike the Senator, however, the VS was only available with American General Motors engines: a 3.8-litre V6, a 5.0-litre V8 and a 5.7-litre V8.

The first models to be launched were the Calais, which was the luxury model, the Acclaim, the Berlina, and the sporty SS. The Statesman, Caprice and Commodore arrived in 1990. The different model designations denoted little more than trim levels. Performance from the top-of-the-range 5.7-litre V8 was astounding, with a top speed approaching 150mph(240km/h) and 60mph (100km/h) arriving in under seven seconds.

Holden held on to its second place among Australian manufacturers, with production figures not far behind those of its age-old rival Ford Australia.

Above: Holden VS Caprice

Below: Holden VS Acclaim

Above: HoldenVS Berlina

Below:: Holden VS Calais

Honda

Japan
1962 to date

The story of Honda is a classic rags-to-riches tale. Born in Iwata-gun, Japan, in 1906, Soichiro Honda was the son of a blacksmith who also repaired bicycles to supplement his income. One of nine children, of whom only four survived, his poor background denied him a formal education, but it did not dampen a spirit of enterprise and adventure, or a fascination for things mechanical.

Inheriting his father's mechanical abilities and helping with his father's main work of repairing implements he recalled years later that he was deeply stirred the first time he saw a car.

Honda joined an automobile repair shop in Tokyo after leaving school, and a few years later with his own capital set up a branch shop at Hamamatsu. He began making cast wheel spokes for cars and went on to the manufacture of piston rings by the time he was 28.

While Honda was apprenticed in Tokyo the city suffered violent earthquakes in 1923. The repair shop was destroyed through subsequent fires, but not before the workers had managed to evacuate the cars they were working on.

The emergency gave Honda his first chance to drive a car and then a motor-cycle and sidecar as he ferried people about and picked up provisions in the earthquake's aftermath. Most cars at the time had wooden spoked wheels and many were burnt away in the fires. This gave him the idea to make a better alternative in the form of metal wheels.

Meanwhile, Honda was busy learning the skills and developing resourcefulness for all aspects of vehicle repair. With parts in short supply he had to improvise. These years formed a thorough grounding from which he was to achieve success beyond imagination.

There can be little doubt that his progress would have been swifter had it not been for the Japanese tradition of seniority. Owners preferred to entrust their cars to older mechanics. Honda had to take on the cars that others said were hopeless cases, and his genius in getting these cars back into service won him the respect he deserved.

Having started his own shop with one assistant it was not long before he had built his business into a 50-man operation. His profits allowed him to indulge in some of life's luxuries. He took up speedboat racing and began to look closely at racing cars. He had already worked on preparing a racing car with his Tokyo employer Shin'ichi Sakakibara while apprenticed. Working in his own time during 1925 he helped build the machine using an 8.2-litre Curtis aircraft engine. The car was a race-winner, but Honda never drove it.

It was in 1935, the year he married, that Honda came back to the sport, this time as a driver using Ford power. His exploits in this respect were short-lived, however. A serious crash in 1936 ended his ambitions. While leading the All-Japan Speed Rally on a circuit between Tokyo and Yokohama a car moved into his path.

In the resulting crash Honda's car somersaulted three times and he did not recover consciousness until he was in hospital. The left side of his face was crushed, his left arm dislocated and his left wrist broken. It took him 18 months to recover.

Now looking for a new direction, Honda decided to go into manufacture. He applied himself to the study of casting so that he could make piston rings. It meant going back to school, for the subject was not as simple as he had at first supposed, and he almost drained his company of money because of the time taken and mistakes made before he was able to make rings of acceptable quality.

He beat the problem and even designed a machine to make rings automatically, and for Japan's war effort he produced a machine which could make an aircraft bomber propeller in 30 minutes. Until then it had required a week of manual labour.

When the war finished Honda could see the urgent need for cheap personal transport as the population tried to pick up the threads of civilian life. He started the Honda Technical Research Laboratory in 1946 having hit upon the idea of fitting small military engines, used for generators and radios, to bicycles. Petrol was in short supply, so cars were a luxury, and buses and trains were overcrowded.

With help from a younger brother, Benjiro, and Kiyoshi Kawashima (who was to become company president) Honda produced a motor-cycle entirely of his own manufacture in 1949. He called it the Dream because of his dream for speed.

The Honda story might have been different had Takeo Fujisawa not come

along. He became Honda's right-hand man, guiding the business, handling the marketing and generating fresh ideas.

In 1950 Honda and Fujisawa opened an office in Tokyo, the centre of finance and manufacturing in Japan. The following year Honda produced his first four-stroke engine. Kawashima test-rode the new model. They were thrilled with its performance and in 1952 Honda was awarded the Blue Ribbon Medal for inventions and improvements to small engines.

The company went on to become the world's biggest manufacturer of motorcycles, and it still holds that distinction today.

It was not until 1963 that the first Honda four-wheeled passenger vehicle was introduced. The previous year Honda had constructed a small sports car, the S360, with chain-drive to both rear wheels. It never went into production, but it was displayed at the 1962 Tokyo Show as a statement of intent.

The company's first four-wheeled production vehicle was a truck using the same twin-cam four-cylinder 360cc engine. This was launched in August 1963, followed in October by the 500cc version of the Tokyo Show sports car.

Below: 1963 Honda 500cc S500

Above: 1965 L700 Estate

The four-carburettor S500 was replaced in March 1964 by the S600 with a conventional rear axle instead of dual chains, and in January 1966 the S800, the first Honda car to arrive in Britain, was launched.

Quick to perceive a home market for small fuel-efficient cars as workers were beginning to enjoy higher standards of living, Honda introduced the N360 four-stroke twin-cylinder microcar. It took the Japanese market by storm in 1967.

By that time Honda had been making a name for itself on the world car-racing scene. The company's first race was the German round of the Formula One series in August 1964 with a 1.5-litre V12.

It was in Germany the following year that an S600 Coupé won its class in an endurance race at the Nürburgring. Honda's first F1 win was also in 1965, the

Mexico Grand Prix in October with Richie Ginther at the wheel. This was the first F1 victory by a Japanese car.

The following year the F1 class was changed to an engine capacity of three litres. Honda built another V12 and with it John Surtees won the 1967 Italian GP.

An advocate of air-cooled engines, Honda persuaded his company to try this type and for 1968 a 120-degree V12 version producing 430bhp was produced, a very powerful machine for its time. Tragically, Jo Schlesser was killed at the French GP in the RA301 and at the end of 1968 Honda withdrew from two- and four-wheel racing.

Channelling his energies into road cars, Honda set about the problem of pollution. He personally joined the taskforce working

on the CVCC (compound vortex controlled combustion) engine which came to fruition in 1973 and was first used in the Honda Civic. Honda had set up an anti-pollution centre in 1970 and his new engine met the stringent U.S. exhaust emission requirements two years before they became law.

An egalitarian who insisted that all his workers wear a white uniform to emphasize their work as a team, his honest toil nurtured an empire which helped Japan to emerge as the second largest car manufacturing country in the world.

In 1974 at the age of 67 he decided to

Below: 1965 RA 271 Formula One racing car. With this 1.5-litre V12, Honda became the first Japanese manufacturer to win in F1. The four-valve head engine would rev to 13,000rpm. Hi-tech Hondas had arrived.

Top: 1978 example of Honda Civic

Above: 1978 Accord EX-L Saloon

Below: RA 302 Formula One racing car of 1968. This 2988cc 120-degree V8 was air cooled and gave 430bhp. After making a terrific impact in racing on two and four wheels, Honda quit sport at the end of 1968 to concentrate on road vehicles.

Below: 1970 Z Coupé. This 360cc air-cooled four-stroke twin developed 36bhp. A sporty version of the highly successful N360 of 1966, the Z360 was improved by water cooling in 1971. The Japanese home market loved these tiny vehicles.

retire as president and become 'supreme advisor'. Since that time he has quietly guided his various companies as they have set up factories in various parts of the world and provided the horsepower for the public and the Formula One world champions of the 1980s.

In the 1990s, Honda plans to supplement the success of its famously competent and reliable Civic, Accord and Prelude models with cars of a more luxurious or sporty nature. These are being sold in the U.S. through a separate sales channel under the name Acura, a strategy likely to be emulated elsewhere in the world. Acura's first models, the small Integra hatchback and mid-sized Legend

Right: 1985 2.0 Accord Aerodeck
Below right: Ballade for 1985
Far right above: 1986 Integra
Far right bottom: 1986 Honda CRX

Above: 1978 Prelude two-door coupé
Right: Revised Accord of 1982

Above: 1986 Prelude 2.0

Below: Honda's 1978 Prelude evolved into an ingenious four-wheel steering version in 1988. The rear wheels turn the same way as the front at slow speeds and in the opposite direction at higher speeds.

Left: CRX coupé, launched in 1984
Above: 1.4 Civic GL 16-valve

Left: 1987 2.7 Legend coupé
Above: 1990 Civic GL saloon
Below: Concerto, launched in June 1988

Left: Latest version 2.0 injection Accord
Above: 16-valve 1.6i-16 Concerto

Above: Honda Concerto GL

Below: 1984 Honda Civic Shuttle. The estate car of the Civic range with 12-valve 1488cc front-wheel-drive engine, it featured a high roof line and doors extended into the roof area for ease of passenger entry and exit. A small vehicle that is big on space.

Above: 2.2i Accord with sunroof
Right: Twin carburettor Concerto EX

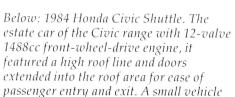

saloon and coupé, soon exceeded U.S. sales targets; the next addition to the range, the 258km/h (160mph) NS-X two-seater launched in 1989, is cause for concern for all Europe's sports car makers.

Right: 2.7 V6 air-conditioned Legend
Below: Four-wheel-drive 1.6 Shuttle
Bottom: Acura mock-up of mid-engined sports car for the U.S. market

The NSX went into production in 1990, and wowed the world. By the end of the 1980s, Honda had built up a reputation for reliable and highly competent cars, but had never really built a supercar.

The NSX used state-of-the-art technology, including a fantastic 274bhp V6 engine featuring Honda's excellent V-TEC variable valve timing. Handling, thanks to a near perfect weight distribution, was excellent. It was soon praised as the easiest supercar to drive but lacked one of the most important elements of a true supercar – passion. It was certainly an almost clinically perfect car, better in many ways than its Italian rivals, but lacking in the kind of kudos held by its competitors. If you've set your heart on a Ferrari or Lamborghini, you're never going to go out and buy a Honda instead.

The rest of the Honda range continued successfully but, due to a rather frumpy

image, those models with a Rover equivalent were often outsold by their British-badged equivalent in Europe

Following BMW's takeover of the British company, Honda lost interest in Rover and its future models look set to separate themselves from those of the British firm.

Top: 1996 Honda Legend

Above: 1997 Honda CRX

Below: Honda Accord

Above: 1997 Honda Civic five-door VTi

Below: Honda Civic three-door

Right: 1997 Honda Civic Coupé

Above: 1997 NSX Targa-top

Below: 1997 Honda CR-V

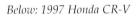

Below: 1996 Honda Prelude 2.2 VTi

Below left: 1990 Honda Legend coupé

Below middle: 1990 Honda Legend saloon

Below: 1997 Honda Shuttle

Horch

Germany
1898–1940

August Horch gained his automotive industry experience as engineering manager with Benz at Mannheim. He left in 1899 to start his own factory in Ehrenfeld, Cologne, backed by a local cloth merchant.

Horch's first car appeared by 1900, and about ten were made. Two years later Horch moved to larger premises at Reichenbach in Vogtland to build bigger models, then in 1904 he went on to Zwickau, Saxony, with a workforce of around 300 as production increased.

In 1906 a Horch car won the Herkomer Trophy and, heartened by this, the company entered a vehicle in the first Prince Henry Trial two years later. Disagreements with his partners over the unsuccessful eight-litre engine of 1906 eventually led to Horch leaving the firm in 1909.

Top right: 1900 4/5hp voiturette
Above: 1906 18/22 model
Right: 1910 31/60 PS six

Over the next five years the extensive Horch range, under technical director Georg Paulmann, went from 1588cc to 6395cc in engine size. In 1920, Horch was taken over by Dr. Moritz Straus of Argus Motoren in Berlin. For the next two years Arnold Zoller was in charge, then Paul Daimler, which saw design improvement. Daimler's influence was still evident in the two models launched after he left the company in 1924.

The Depression seriously affected sales of Horch cars, although they were noted for combining luxury with a comparatively low price. In 1951 Argus sold the Horch factory to Auto-Union, who already owned D.K.W., Wanderer and Audi – the last of which was begun by August Horch when he left the company in 1909.

The Horch works then became home to the Porsche-designed Auto-Union competition cars, under the management of Dr. Richard Bruhn, although the larger Horch cars continued throughout the 1930s. By 1940 production of cars was halted, but some 4×4 command cars were built for the Wehrmacht during World War II using Ford engines.

The name was revived briefly in 1956 for a six-cylinder car produced at Zwickau, but Auto-Union objected and the name was changed to Sachsenring the following year.

The luxurious cars that Horch made during the 1930s, such as this 853, were extremely well built and well engineered, featuring straight-eight engines (apart from a very few V12s) and all-independent suspension.

Top left: August Horch driving a 1914 14/35

Top right: 1931 Type 670 six-litre cabriolet
Above: The V8 range lasted until 1939

Hotchkiss

France
1903–1954

The badge of Hotchkiss features two crossed cannon – entirely appropriate for a firm which started, and was nearly finished by, munitions manufacture.

Though nominally a French company, Hotchkiss had strong links with America and, later, Britain. The firm was started in the 1870s by Benjamin Hotchkiss, an American who had made money supplying shells for the American Civil War but later moved to St. Denis, a suburb of Paris, to set up a factory there for the manufacture of munitions.

However, the skilled precision engineering that was needed to make arms and ammunition proved to be ideal for the burgeoning skill of car manufacture, and during a lull in the world arms market Hotchkiss found itself employed to provide parts to several manufacturers. The logical next step was to produce its own car, which it eventually did in 1903.

In the meantime a major reorganization had taken place; in 1885 Benjamin Hotchkiss had died and another American, Laurence Binet, took the reins, though a takeover by a British consortium happened not long after.

The first all-Hotchkiss car was designed by George Terrasse, who came from the Mors concern, and unsurprisingly it was similar to the contemporary Mors, though a neat round radiator and bonnet made the 17CV Hotchkiss recognizably individual. The following year a young draughtsman, Harry Ainsworth, joined the company – and he was the man who was to guide it for its most important years.

Though the first cars were unexceptional, engineering innovations followed including the famous Hotchkiss Drive, which was a shaft-drive transmission system with a live rear-axle layout. Sales became very respectable, considering that large, luxury cars were the firm's stock-in-trade, and in 1911 the French firm bought out its British board of directors and started making slightly less up-market

Top: 1910 model with distinctive bonnet
Below: 1926 AM2 boat-tail

Above: A well-preserved T type
Below: The AM80S of 1932

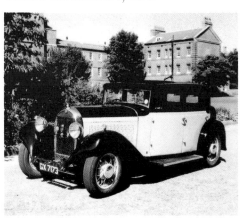

vehicles, though still retaining its reputation for accurate, precise engineering.

During World War I the armaments business flourished, and Hotchkiss acquired two satellite factories, in Coventry and Lyon, to build items like its light machine-gun. After the war the Coventry factory was bought by Morris, the Lyon one by Saurer, and meanwhile Hotchkiss moved itself to a new plant, albeit still in St. Denis.

After the war the company addressed itself firmly to the middle-class market, which proved a wise move. Its aborted AK luxury car, of which only one prototype was ever built, was firmly rejected in favour of the middle-market Type AM which lasted until 1928, when it was replaced by the three-litre AM80 and its sporty 3½-litre AM80S cousin. This proved successful on the track and, most particularly, in rallies like the Monte Carlo, which it won many times.

However, good though it was, that model was to remain, with minor changes, the mainstay of the range until 1950 – becoming an anachronism well before its final end, and that of the company. One example of the firm's intransigence is the fact that it stuck to the tradition of making

The 1936 Grand Sport was powered by a justly famous 3½-litre engine, and gained many notable rallying victories. Its classic lines were elegant when new, but dated badly, particularly as the model was in production for nearly twenty years.

right-hand-drive cars long after every other French company had abandoned the antiquated and inconvenient custom.

The company was hard-hit by the French government's decision to nationalize armaments manufacture in 1936, as the huge losses it incurred were not compensated for until several years later.

World War II was the death knell for Hotchkiss, though it was to struggle on until 1954 with almost non-existent sales. When the Germans invaded France, company head Ainsworth attempted to escape with a convoy of records, supplies and tools but only he himself made it out of the country. The factory was devastated by bombing, and the firm was criticized after the war for not working slowly enough in the German cause and so lost vital reconstruction grants.

Above: Hotchkiss 680 Monte Carlo of 1937
Below: 1938 roadster-bodied 686GS

After the war, the old 3/3½-litre was resuscitated but, already aged, its appeal was strictly limited and sales dwindled almost to nothing until 1954 when, despite mergers with Peugeot and Delahaye, car production ceased. However, U.S.-designed Jeeps were made, as were trucks, until the 1970s.

H.R.G.

Great Britain
1936–1956

Never in any way interested in volume manufacture of standard family saloons, H.R.G. was one of those classic English companies which survived by catering entirely for the lunatic fringe of flat-capped stringback-gloved sports-car fanatics.

Like Morgan, Squire and Lotus, H.R.G. was started by enthusiasts; in this case a trio comprised of racing drivers E. A. Halford and Guy Robins, and car builder H. R. 'Dan' Godfrey, who had previously been responsible, with Archie Frazer-Nash, for the first real sporting light car, the G.N. in 1910.

It was 1935 when the three established their workshop at Norbiton in Surrey, though they were to move a year later to nearby Tolworth. They took a 1500cc four-cylinder Meadows engine which had the benefit of being tuneable to produce a

very respectable power output, and built around it a car which was lightweight and had, by the standards of the day, extremely impressive handling.

The suspension could by no manner of means be described as comfortable, but allowed precise, controllable handling. There was room for two people, but you

Above: 1936 Meadows-engined 1½-litre

would have to be fairly close friends, and luxuries like heating, adequate weather-proofing and so on were strictly not on the menu.

But what the H.R.G. did offer was a feast for the enthusiast; a car equally at home in a variety of motor sports and which gave unmatched driving thrills and

The 1500 was the epitome of H.R.G. motoring, and as such the epitome of sporting British motoring both before and immediately after World War II. The cars may have been primitive but they were fast and handled well for their era.

responsive handling in any situation. Acceleration was excellent and, though the cable-operated brakes were primitive, they were effective – and adjustable while on the move.

The Meadows engine was replaced a few years later by Singer units of either one- or 1½-litre capacity, highly tuned by H.R.G. themselves. With these engines, the formerly competitive cars became even more impressively quick, winning their class at Le Mans, taking similar successes in rallies like the Alpine Rally and the RAC Rally, and were rarely out of the winners list in innumerable club hill-climbs, sprints and trials.

A milestone, though a rather lumpy one, was claimed in 1947 with the Aerodynamic model; it was the first British production sports car with full-width bodywork, which makes it something of a pioneer. However, its upright windscreen and extra weight meant that it was little faster than the normal model and it was soon withdrawn from the range.

In 1955 a new model featuring much new-fangled technology (tubular space frame structure, independent suspension and disc brakes) appeared.

This was again built around a Singer engine, and Singer themselves were getting quite interested in the idea of much closer collaboration with H.R.G., possibly including taking over the new model's manufacture and utilizing the smaller firm's tuning expertise to liven up standard Singers. However, the Rootes Group bought Singer and blocked the collaboration. Within a year the 'classic' H.R.G. had ceased production – again, partly due to Rootes' decision to discontinue the Singer SM1500 engine which was by then H.R.G.'s chosen powerplant.

The firm itself had over the years become run more and more by company secretary Grace Leather, who was sole proprietor by the time it stopped trading in 1966. By that time, however, it had been for some years merely a light-engineering and tuning-equipment company. Sadly, a prototype spaceframed sports car based around a Ford Cortina and later a Vauxhall VX4/90 engine, first shown in 1965, was abandoned on the demise of the firm. H. R. Godfrey himself died in 1968 aged 81, after a long illness.

Above: A 1939 H.R.G.
Below: 1940 Aerodynamic prototype

Bottom: In 1948 some of the mechanicals had undergone refinement

Hudson

U.S.A.
1909–1957

In 1909 the Hudson Motor Car Company, destined to become one of America's largest and most important car manufacturers during the 1920s and 1930s, was formed by a small group of people, mainly engineers, headed by Joseph L. Hudson, the owner of a large Detroit department store. Their first car, the 20bhp 2534cc four-cylinder Model 20, was launched in the same year and despite its completely orthodox design (by Howard Coffin) it became an instant best seller.

Below: Early Hudsons, such as this Hudson 37 of 1913, had four-cylinder engines. Six-cylinder machines followed with four-speed overdrive transmission.

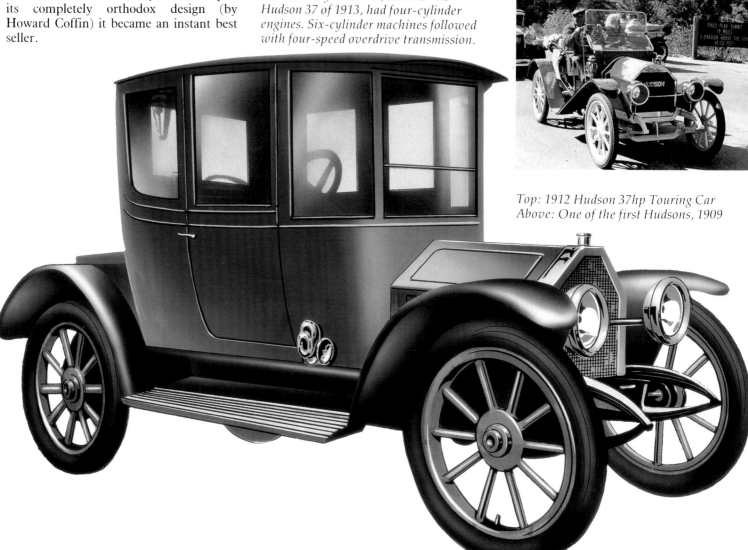

Top: 1912 Hudson 37hp Touring Car
Above: One of the first Hudsons, 1909

Sadly 1912 saw the death of Joseph Hudson, but the birth of Hudson's first six-cylinder car, the Model 6-54, a large and handsome machine powered by a six-litre 54bhp engine. It was built in a range of both open and closed body styles and by 1914 the company was proclaiming itself to be the world's largest manufacturer of six-cylinder cars.

In 1916 the four-cylinder engines were dropped and the company adopted a one-model policy beginning with the Super-Six whose 4739cc engine remained virtually unchanged right through the 1930s. There was a wide range of body styles including sedans, cabriolets, limousines and tourers, and the car was an instant success, with President Hoover taking delivery of a Super-Six Landaulet.

In order to increase its market share, Hudson introduced in 1919, under the 'Essex' name, a less-expensive line of cars

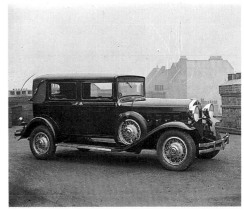

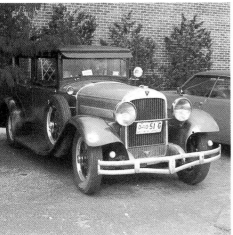

Above: 1929 Hudson Superb Sedan

Top: Enrico Caruso and a 1920 Hudson Super Six Limousine (Montreal)
Above: 1925 Hudson Phaeton

Above: 1929 Hudson Super Eight

Below: 1934 Hudson Six

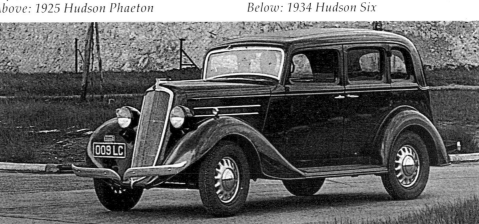

powered by a 2.9-litre four-cylinder and later 2.6-litre six-cylinder engines in a range of body styles. During the peak years of 1925–29 the sales of the Essex cars greatly exceeded those of the parent company and by 1929 the Essex-Hudson combination was rated third-best seller in the U.S.A.

Another important landmark was the introduction of a straight-eight-engined car in 1930, with the engine remaining in production until 1953 by which time the power had been gradually increased from 95bhp at 3,500rpm to 128bhp at 4,200rpm. Body styles were regularly updated to compete with the big three – Ford, General Motors and Chrysler – although during the late 1930s production (and profits) ebbed and flowed with a trading loss in 1939 and 1940, followed by a small profit the following year.

After the demise of the Essex line in 1932 the Hudson and Essex Terraplane cars became almost indistinguishable. In 1935 a novel electric gear shift, the 'Electric Hand', became available as an

Below left: Four-door Hudson sedan of 1934

Above: 1935 Hudson Custom Brougham
Below: 1940 Hudson Super 6

Below: The Hudson Essex Town Sedan was a graceful machine with flowing wings. The combination of Hudson and Essex gave sales success in the late 1920s.

Left: 1946 Hudson 6-20 model

Above: 1946 Hudson ¾ ton Pick-up

Centre left: 1949 Hudson Superb
Centre right: 1950 Hudson Pacemaker
Above: 1953 Hudson Hornet

Right: 1954 prototype Hudson Italia

option, while in 1936 the 'safety engineered chassis' was developed with Bendix hydraulic brakes backed up by a mechanical system should the hydraulics fail.

During World War II the Hudson factory was turned over to manufacturing war materials and machines and it was not until 1948 that the company launched its new unitary-construction 'Step-Down Design' body-chassis unit in which one stepped down over the structural body sills on to the lowered floor. The new car line-up included the lower-priced Pacemakers with 3.8-litre 112bhp six-cylinder engines, and the top-of-the-range Commodore Eights with their 4168cc 128bhp units.

In the early 1950s sales were flagging again despite the supremacy of the five-litre Hornet in stock-car racing and the announcement of the compact 3.3-litre Jet in 1953. The latter was abandoned the following year when Hudson merged with Nash to form American Motors, and by 1957 the Hudson name had disappeared.

Below: 1942 Hudson H21 sedan

Top: 1951 Hudson Pacemaker Convertible   *Below: 1957 Hudson Hollywood*

Left: 1948 Hudson sedan

Above: 1951 Hudson Commodore 8

Index